DECOUPAGE
A Practical Guide

DECOUPAGE
A Practical Guide

DECORATING WITH PAPER CUT-OUTS

Audrey Raymond

CASSELL

A CASSELL BOOK
First published in the UK
1993 by Cassell
Villiers House
41/47 Strand
London
WC2N 5JE

First published in 1993 by
Simon & Schuster Australia
20 Barcoo Street, East Roseville NSW 2069

Copyright © 1993 Audrey Raymond

British Library Cataloguing-in-Publication Data
A catalogue record for this book is available from the
British Library
ISBN 0 304 34349 8

Designed by Anna Warren
Typeset by Asset Typesetting Pty Ltd in Sydney, Australia
Printed and bound by South China Printing Co. Ltd.

Contents

Acknowledgements **6**

Introduction **8**

1 History and Styles **10**

2 Materials — Information and Use **16**

3 Tips and Techniques **22**

4 Design **31**

5 Basic Découpage Under Varnish **36**

6 Découpage Under Glass **47**

7 Lining a Box **54**

8 Cloisonné and Illumination **58**

9 Hand Colouring **64**

10 Repoussé, Moulage and Tôle **72**

11 Other Projects **78**

12 A Whole New World **86**

Glossary **88**

Brand Names of Materials **91**

Bibliography **92**

Index **93**

Acknowledgements

The greatest pleasure I have derived from writing this book is the knowledge that I am able to thank my many inspiring American teachers, and my fellow découpeurs, both in the United States and elsewhere, whom I have been privileged to meet and number amongst my friends. My deep appreciation of their kindness, trust in me and warmth of their friendship can never be adequately expressed. Those who taught me gave their time, hospitality, skill and effort in boundless measure. All I have been able to do in return is to try to duplicate their high standards, knowledge and sense of generosity to my own students.

Most of my knowledge has been acquired from what I have read or gleaned from my teachers in the United States, together, of course, with what I have learned from trial and error. I am also not ashamed to admit that my pupils are a never-ending source of inspiration, which makes teaching such a joy.

I wish to convey my sincerest thanks and affection to the following people to whom I owe so much: my dear friend Gene Clockman (not forgetting Leon), who first invited me to Dallas to share all she could with me in three weeks; Ann Standish, the greatly valued Secretary of the National Guild of Découpeurs (America), an endless source of assistance to me as well as being a kind hostess and friend, along with her husband Bill.

Then there are the talented teachers and découpeurs, Carol Perry and Joanne Sartor, with whom I had many happy and informative hours.

Others who gave of their knowledge, hospitality and time were Roberta Raffaelli and the late Marie Mitchell, who touched me greatly by giving me fascinating individual instruction when she was in great pain from her final illness.

It goes without saying that I was privileged and thrilled to be able to spend a day with Hiram Manning, the doyen of découpage, during which time he opened my eyes to his breathtaking skill with scissors and hand-colouring.

Two other distinguished Guild members whose interest and encouragement has been greatly appreciated are Joy Allbright and Adele McGilvray.

While I owe so much to the teachers who changed my life, I must equally thank the many students with whom I have been associated. Their enthusiasm and support, along with the pleasure they have derived from what they have learnt is a source of constant pleasure to me.

Mention must be made of Nerida Singleton, whose beautiful Victorian-style découpage and classes have done much to stimulate and spread an interest in découpage throughout Australia, to the benefit of us all.

The Découpage Guild Australia Inc., based in Melbourne, sports an active group of members who produce imaginative and creative découpage of the highest standard.

I am very proud of the work some of my students have produced for this book and warmly thank them for their contributions. They are Lola McNickle (p. 45, gold braid box; p. 83, egg; p. 84, gold-leaf transparency box), Nerida Cullen (p. 62, triptych screen; p. 78, silhouettes), Dorothy White (p. 45, matching small box and handmirror; p. 76, writing box and plaque), Sue Blinkhorn (p. 71), Judith Luget (p. 83, shells except for small shell pendants; p. 84, crackle-finish box on right), June Cooper (p. 76, tôle shoe and round box), Margaret Fink (p. 44, open box), Faye Furse (p. 52, plate far left), Kristine Bowden (p. 45, octagonal box), Phyllis Cant (p. 52, second plate from left), and Mark Hughes for his fine cutting. (All other pieces created by the author.)

I am also delighted and grateful to have been able to include photos of the work of Philippa Barbour, Joy Allbright, Joanne Sartor, Val Lade and a number of the very talented members of the National Guild of Découpeurs in America.

I cannot imagine how I could have coped without the considerable help and generosity of Guy Kingdon, Milka Bogovitch, Gillian Reckitt and June Ohlson, whose practical support so greatly eased the challenge of producing this book.

Introduction

'Welcome to a whole new world!' Those were the introductory words at my first découpage lesson with Gene Clockman, my distinguished teacher in Dallas, USA. I have remembered them ever since for I did enter a whole new world as have many others who, like me, have discovered découpage.

Découpage is the traditional art of decorating surfaces with cut out paper compositions. Découpage is not montage, attractive as this method of paper manipulation is. Découpage involves many different techniques (including répoussé and moulage, hand-colouring, illumination, cloisonné and gold leaf transparency) on many different surfaces from wood and glass to silk, porcelain, pottery, shells, metals and plastic. It is an art form that combines the decorative and the useful.

Découpage is a most exciting and absorbing skill that appeals to people of all ages and walks of life. It develops their latent artistic talent and challenges their patience and imagination. It leads them to discover depths of creativity, which they often never knew they possessed.

It is a sharing pastime. If we are to grow and develop in this exciting art form and keep it alive, we must stimulate and create interest and admiration for the art, and constantly be developing and sharing new techniques and ideas without losing the essence of its traditional form. It is only through the generosity of others that we each glean what knowledge we have, and we should perpetuate this spirit of giving. There is plenty of room for us all, to produce our own unique creations, thereby allowing découpage to remain a living, vibrant art form.

Many people have gone before me and much of great interest has already been written, but there is always room for more. In *Traditional Découpage* my aim has been to make available as much information as is necessary to set you on the right road to this new and exciting world of découpage, and to be a source of additional ideas for those who are already experienced but perhaps need reassurance or some fresh inspiration. It therefore includes a variety of techniques aimed to stimulate the découpeur who is confident about the basic steps and wants to move on to new pastures.

However, I particularly want to open doors for the beginner, and so I have aimed to keep the explanations of the techniques simple to avoid being too daunting for those who wish to teach themselves. From chapter 5 on, each chapter covers a different technique, and is devoted to leading you through the various steps of découpage, including photographs to help you on your way.

This may be your first attempt at découpage. Set out to enjoy it — you have lots of thrills and spills in store. While you are absorbed in découpage you will never have a dull moment. Naturally, learning a new skill will not always be a bed of roses but remember that if you have a disaster, or something you *think* is a disaster, rest assured it is unlikely to be insurmountable. Very few problems cannot be rectified, not even inadvertently cooking a box on a hotplate of a stove just after it has been finished so that the prints burn and the varnish melts! Don't panic, just look up your problem in this book — along with some reassuring words, it is sure to mention somewhere how to deal with the crisis. You will find particular help in chapter 2 (*Materials — Information and Use*), chapter 3 (*Tips and Techniques*) and chapter 4 (*Design*). The main thing is that découpage is fun and very rewarding. You will also earn the praise of many admirers marvelling at the effects you achieve!

You don't have to spend a fortune to enjoy découpage, and more importantly you don't have to be able to draw or paint in order to make an object of great beauty and skill. As long as you enjoy colour and design and have a desire to create something, then découpage is for you.

A common remark is 'Oh, I wouldn't have the patience'. Well lots of people have surprised themselves by unexpectedly discovering they have hidden depths of patience they did not know they possessed.

Découpage is an absorbing and rewarding pastime which has given an enormous amount of pleasure to many people, and can even be said to be therapeutic!

One of the most exciting aspects of this art form is its limitless potential for new creative ideas — you can experiment continually with new techniques. Be warned, however, you will become a paper junkie! You will find it impossible to pass newsagents, bookshops, craft shows, galleries, markets, bric-à-brac stalls and antiques shops without popping in — just in case! Soon one of the rooms of your house will be taken over to store all your papers, paints, varnishes, boxes and the like. At Christmas you will eye your friends' cards in an acquisitive manner, and soon after you will be demanding first refusal of everybody's decorative calendars from the previous year.

One thing that you should remember is that while in découpage you may use other people's designs in your work, for example, prints, illustrations and photographs, *you* are creating an original and unique design and composition, not just transposing the work of another artist on to the object you are decorating. It is the way *you* compose the prints that makes the work uniquely yours. Develop the design to suit the shape of the article you are embellishing or, if necessary, to fill an unwanted space. Snip off a bit here, add a bit there, and combine a print elsewhere. Be adventurous and innovative. This is the essence of creative découpage.

1

History and Styles

Découpage is a creative, decorative and timeless art form with its roots in the Venice of 300 years ago. Découpage is the art of adorning surfaces with paper cut-outs to form a complete design or to tell a story, and the techniques for achieving this are limitless. The word *découpage* was derived from the French word *découper*, meaning to cut out.

In the past découpage has been known by many names. The Italians referred to it as *art povera* or *art del povera* (poor man's art), or *lacche povero* (poor man's lacquer) and *lacche contrafatta* (simulated lacquer). The French called it *lacque pauvre* (again, poor man's lacquer) or *l'art scriban*, a term still used in France today. In England it was known as *japanning* because it emulated the lacquer work which came to Europe from Japan and China in the eighteenth century.

The origin of découpage as we know it today dates back to seventeenth-century Italy when cabinet-makers were keen to copy this Far Eastern lacquer work because of its immense popularity. They used cut-out prints, engravings or lithographs which were hand-coloured and positioned on painted backgrounds. These were then coated with lacquer to give the appearance of genuine Eastern lacquer work.

Rich citizens of that era employed master painters to decorate their ceilings, walls and furniture. The demand for their talents became so great that apprentices were employed to hand-colour prints and engravings of their work which were then stuck on to various surfaces and 'sunk' under layers of lacquer to give the impression of being original paintings. Those who were unable to afford the master painters, employed lesser artists to decorate their houses in this manner.

In addition, découpage is also believed to have been influenced by paper cutting techniques used by the ancient Chinese, felt appliqué work found amongst the peoples of Siberia, and the Polish folk art skill of paper cutting.

While this creative technique was developing in Italy, it was simultaneously becoming fashionable in France where ladies in the French court became keen découpeurs. Young blades and ladies sat snipping away at original works of Boucher, Redouté, Fragonard, Watteau and Pillement to decorate fans, boxes, fire screens, secretaires and the like. Indeed both

A magnificent Roman bureau, dated c. 1750 and decorated in *lacca contrafatta*, depicting some 650 human and animal figures. The bureau is first thought to have belonged to Pope Pius VI. It was then owned by the Grimaldi family and finally moved to the Maillat Collection in Paris. Photograph kindly lent by Pelham Galleries, London.

Marie Antoinette and Madame de Pompadour avidly practised this art form.

These artists are still favourites with today's découpeurs. Boucher's romantic semi-clad women, together with his charming playful cherubs were, and still are, loved by découpeurs. Redouté was famous for his magnificent flower paintings, in particular his roses and lilies. He was patronised first by Marie Antoinette and later by the Empress Josephine, both of whom commissioned him to paint for them.

Classic découpage of eighteenth-century France was particularly influenced by things Chinese. This led to the development of *chinoiserie*, the romantic European interpretation of Chinese styles. Pillement, in particular, reflected this interest. His drawings were imaginative fantasies with a flavour of the Orient, with illustrations of luxuriant vegetation, Chinese figures and fanciful characters as well as delicate birds and feathery flowers. These reflected his love of whimsy and his desire to charm and entertain. Like Redouté, he also worked for Marie Antoinette at the Petit Trianon and was appointed Court Painter.

Another term used for a style of drawings during that period is *singerie*, which comes from the French word *le singe* meaning monkey. These were fanciful illustrations of monkeys and also showed an influence stemming from the Orient.

In the eighteenth century travel was slow and uncomfortable, so when people undertook journeys to visit friends and relations they would stay some time. It was not uncommon for them to take découpage to help pass the time, much as embroidery did, and indeed a thoughtful hostess would often provide paper and a project for decoration to amuse her guests.

Also at that period there lived in London a printer by the name of Robert Sayer. Around 1760 he produced his first edition of *The Ladies Amusement or Whole Art of Japanning Made Easy*, a delightful and innovative book for that time, consisting of 1500

Classical eighteenth-century découpage under varnish. Photograph kindly lent by the National Guild of Découpeurs (USA).

fascinating illustrations and designs which were meant for use by artist craftsmen of the day. There were many drawings of Oriental figures, landscapes, flowers, trees, butterflies and birds by Pillement and others, which were meant for use on textiles, ceramics, enamels, silver and tapestries. However, as the name indicates, the book was also popular with eighteenth-century women who loved to colour and snip away at the enchanting drawings contained within it. The book even describes how the drawings should be coloured. Of special interest to découpeurs is the description of the technique of how to cut out these drawings: 'The Several Objects you intend for Use must be neatly cut round with Scisars, or the small Point of a Knife; those Figures must be brush'd over on the Back with Strong Gum-water, or thin Paste, made by boiling Flour in Water.'

Mention must be made of Mrs Delaney, who lived in eighteenth-century England and attended the court of King George III and Queen Charlotte. The friend of many famous people of the day, such as Hogarth, Swift, Sir Joshua Reynolds, Horace Walpole and Fanny Burney, she was a charming, intelligent and talented lady. At the age of 72, she started to create exquisite, detailed and accurate flower pictures, cut free-hand from thin tissue paper, which she first coloured and then pasted one layer upon the other to produce delicate and botanically correct pictures. Because of the accuracy of her work, she was in great demand by the aristocracy, many of whom imported rare plants from the New World and wanted them recorded for posterity. She also undertook work for the Royal Botanical Gardens at Kew and became a close friend of Sir Joseph Banks. Considering her age (she was productive until she was 82), the materials she used and the times in which she lived, the fineness of her work is extolled by all who see it. It is now housed in the British Museum in London. In addition to her flowers she was very skilled at creating silhouettes.

About 170 years ago a young English invalid called Amelia Blackburn drew, coloured and then cut out the most delicate garlands of flowers, birds and other objects of nature, with great accuracy and trueness to life. She overcame her disability and with great dexterity produced unique work such as the feathers of a bird so fine that they could barely be seen by the naked eye. Her work is known as 'Amelias'. Although neither Amelia nor Mrs Delaney lacquered their work, they both lived at a time when the popularity of découpage was at its height, and there is no doubt that their use

Modern Victorian-style découpage by Nerida Singleton.

of scissors was encouraged by and grew from the popular practice of cutting and lacquering that was being intricately and painstakingly produced in England. Certainly their work still draws great admiration for its technical skill and composition from modern day découpeurs.

So découpage spread throughout Europe, gradually developing various national style characteristics. Patricia Nimmocks, a distinguished American découpeur, identified in her book the variety of styles in different countries. Sicily, for example, produces a gay profusion of decorations depicting religious and historical scenes to adorn festival carts; in Sweden colours are muted and used with black, white and earthy sombre tones on dark backgrounds. Norwegian découpage is nearly all confined to subjects of mythology and the Vikings. Belgians tend to limit themselves to producing silhouettes; while Portuguese découpage is bright and sparkling and employs foil and tinsel paper.

It could be said découpage reached its zenith in Victorian England, and Queen Victoria became an enthusiastic collector. However, the art was somewhat debased by losing its delicacy and sophistication because the women of the day used whole pictures, with the minimum of cutting out. With these they decorated screens, hat boxes, writing slopes, trays, glove boxes and other household and domestic objects. Valentine and greeting cards, scrapbook pictures, magazine cuttings, pre-coloured and embossed papers, and gold paper braids were used extensively, as were early photographs. As was typical of the Victorian era, items produced at this time tended to be cluttered, sentimental and rather heavy in form, but at the same time had a boldness, colour and charm of their own. In recent years, this style of découpage has had a considerable revival in popularity. Victorian découpage techniques introduced the use of pre-coloured prints and photographs as we use them today.

In Paris in the 1920s, the French Art Deco designer Jean-Michel Frank decorated his famous tables with paper cut-outs. Everyone at some time or another must have seen the work of the artist Matisse, whose famous pictures of paper cut-outs were the major creations of his later years. Picasso also used découpage techniques in some of his works. And in the 1930s the distinguished *Vogue* editor Caroline Duer created magnificent découpage in the slightly heavy Biedermeier style using figures, flowers, garlands and embossed papers and braids on boxes and furniture. Her

The interior of a trunk. Découpage showing creative cutting and applied to a fabric surface with mother-of-pearl inlay. Created by Joanne Sartor.

work may be seen in a number of private collections and museums throughout the United States.

Currently découpage is practised all over the world with particularly skilled and creative work coming from the United States, Canada, Japan, Korea, Australia, South Africa and the United Kingdom. Considering its past, it is surprising that there is not such a strong following in Europe at present although découpage is still being produced commercially in Italy.

No book should be written today without mentioning the work of The National Guild of Découpeurs, founded in the United States in 1971 'to distinguish découpage as an art form in itself'. It is the Guild that is greatly responsible for keeping alive an interest in this skilled and exquisite art form and for maintaining its traditional techniques 'while inspiring and enthusing exponents of découpage around the world'.

In the twentieth century one name has been synonymous with découpage, that of Hiram Manning. He learnt what was becoming a dying art form at the time from a French family when he stayed with them in their richly decorated Normandy manor and brought it back to Boston around 1930. There he and his mother, May-belle, began to teach, employing the highest standards, and his enthusiasm and knowledge spread to such an extent that today America is the home of some of the finest découpage.

Even now the work of many serious découpeurs is still influenced by the eighteenth century, as reproductions of eighteenth-century prints are used profusely and are still hand-coloured providing a more classical découpage

Découpage using hand-coloured Pillement illustrations. Created by a member of the National Guild of Decoupeurs (USA).

Vue d'optique. Three-dimensional découpage showing a moonlit scene fading into infinity. Created by a member of the National Guild of Découpeurs (USA).

flavour. The Oriental influence is also seen in the application of *chinoiserie* prints by modern day exponents of this art. Nineteenth-century paintings are also popular particularly with Victorian-influenced work, and more recently the works of Matisse, Gaugin, Dali and others are used in modern compositions. Following the tradition of silhouettes, the National Guild of Découpeurs has encouraged the skill of creative cutting where the découpeur does not have a drawing to cut out but must create a free-cut design.

Today contemporary designs have found their way into much of modern découpage with pleasing effect. Many découpeurs now use pre-coloured wrapping papers, art books, cards and calendars. Some more adventurous exponents have used insects' wings, fish scales, the skeletons of dead leaves and even a cobweb with their prints. The recent revival of interest in faux finishes, eggshell inlay and gold and silver leaf has provided interesting alternative backgrounds to basic painted, limed or stained surfaces on which to apply the prints. The possibilities for making decorator items, both traditional and modern, are numerous.

The possibilities for découpage are limitless for decorator items, furniture, objets d'art and jewellery. It can be applied to a number of different surfaces, ranging from timber to glass, ceramics, tin, eggs, fabric, plastic, stone, shells and soap.

Apart from prints being 'sunk' on flat surfaces, they can be applied under glass, used with coloured foil in the techniques known as cloisonné and illumination, or raised and moulded as in repoussé, moulage and tôle. They can be cut in such a way as to be elevated and made three-dimensional. These 'elevations', and their related *vue d'optique*, have their origins in the peep shows of the nineteenth century where little scenes and vistas, made from stand-up paper, could be viewed through a small aperture — a secret world!

2

Materials – Information and Use

The information in this chapter is provided as a general guideline to the use of different materials, which are listed in alphabetical order. Remember, though, that exceptions or alternatives can apply to many of the rules. Besides, innovations are constantly being introduced, changes are being made to the make-up of substances and new materials are coming on to the market. Découpeurs often develop strong likes and dislikes for different materials and the way they are used, so there are few hard and fast rules. In time you will develop your own preferences but for now this information should act as a good starting point.

COLOUR PENCILS

Use oil-based pencils such as Derwent, Prismacolour or Faber Castell Polychromas. Do not use watercolour pencils (aquarelle) because you cannot achieve the same depth of colour, they can run when wet and are more inclined to fade.

GESSO

Gesso is used to fill in the grain of wood and other imperfections. A substance traditionally made from whiting and rabbit skin glue, it has been in use for thousands of years. You may have noticed it as a white substance under a chipped picture or mirror frame since it is an essential base for gilding because it sands to a superb, silky, porcelain-like finish. Synthetic acrylic gesso is now available from art supply shops. As well as being a woodfiller, it is also used in découpage as a background for découpage under glass.

For the best results, stir well and apply 5–6 coats to your surface, brushing it on as smoothly as possible with long firm strokes. Allow to dry well, probably at least 3 hours. A good test to check if it is dry is to hold it against your cheek — if it is cold it is still damp, but if it is body temperature, you're okay! Lightly dry sand between coats and *lightly* wipe with your tack cloth (see page 25).

After the final coat, dip a 400 wet-and-dry sandpaper in water and wet sand the surface, but don't be too fierce. Make sure you keep your sandpaper really wet as you proceed, but do keep wiping the surface with a dry cloth to stop the area becoming too soggy. Keep sanding and wiping and very soon you will have a superb porcelain-like finish — don't stop until

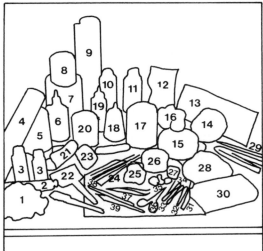

1. Padding 2. Jo Sonia paint 3. Americana paint 4. Wet-and-dry sandpaper 5. Matisse Gesso 6. Aquadhere PVA glue 7. Wattyl Estapol Speed Clear 8. Feast Watson Varnish 9. Wax paper 10. Shines Shellac 11. Liquitex Gloss Medium and Varnish 12. Polycell paper paste 13. Bostik Blu-Tack 14. Kitten Cutting Compound 15. Liberon Wax Polish 16. 0000 steel/wire wool 17. Wattyl Sanding Sealer 18. Clag paste 19. Aleene's Tacky Glue 20. Selley's Wood Stop 21. Tack cloth 22. Polybrushes 23. Brayer/roller 24. Paint brushes 25. Sea sponge 26. The Master's

Brush Cleaner 27. Gum eraser 28. Dust mask 29. Derwent artists' pencils 30. DAS modelling material 31. Wooden spatula 32. Tortillon 33. Cotton tips 34. Toothpick 35. Brass fittings 36. Curved scissors 37. Tweezers 38. Burnisher 39. X-Acto knife

---

all tiny ridges and pits are gone.

You can add acrylic paint to your gesso, which will give it a soft colour and save you having to paint over the gesso later. Gesso can also be used as a white background on its own, but always put a coat of sealer over it before gluing down your prints (see page 41).

Note: You do not need to seal your wood surface before you apply gesso as it is a sealer in itself.

MOULDING MATERIAL

The moulding material for repoussé is also sometimes referred to as *mastic*. It comes in various forms, similar to plasticene, clay or dough. If you cannot get hold of a suitable ready-made material it is possible to make your own in the following ways:

a. 1 cup of cornflour (it *must* be pure cornflour and not wheaten flour)
1 cup of bicarbonate of soda
1 small cup of water (approx. 150 mL)

Combine all ingredients and boil for 5 minutes, stirring all the time. Allow to cool in the pan then roll into a ball and store in the refrigerator, not the freezer. It should last for about five months.

b. *Bread Dough:*
2 slices of white bread, crusts removed

2 tablespoons of white glue
½ tablespoon of glycerin

Knead in a plastic bag until completely smooth.

Do not use home-made recipes too moist because they will shrink when dried, causing your lovely moulded print to end up looking like a dried prune!

OIL AND WATER

Remember this important general rule: Oil goes over water, but water doesn't go over oil. (However, you may use shellac in between the two as an isolator.) In other words, do not try to put a water-based varnish over an oil-based varnish, although the reverse is okay. The same rule applies to paints.

PAINTS

As with varnishes, paints can be either water-based, such as acrylics, or oil-based, and their relationship to each other is the same as the varnishes discussed above.

Water-based paints

Acrylics are clean, easy to use and quick drying. If necessary they can be thinned with water, and water is used for cleaning up. However, they are not as ideal on glass as oil paints since they do not adhere as well and can sometimes crack.

Oil paints

Oil paints take longer to dry, but have a greater depth, are more durable and adhere to glass better than acrylics. Remember that unless you use shellac, you cannot always satisfactorily apply a water-based varnish over them.

SANDPAPERS

Wet-and-dry sandpapers are normally used in découpage and as the name indicates, they can be used in either form. They are black (being made from carbide) and come with a number on the back. The lower the number, the coarser the sandpaper. In general, begin with 400 and finish with 1000 or 1200. When preparing a wood surface the sandpaper is used dry. It is also used dry when sanding very lightly between coats of gesso or paint.

After the final coat of gesso, and once starting varnishing, always use the sandpaper very wet. Put detergent in the water, froth it up and run the sandpaper through the foam. With frequent use sandpaper will get clogged up, and that is the time to throw it away — it's a waste of energy to be mean with it!

Other sandpapers sometimes used for coarser sanding are glass and garnet paper.

SEALERS

Sealers come in different forms. Gesso (see page 16) is a sealer used to obtain a porcelain-smooth finish on a surface you wish to decorate. Shellac (see below) is another. However, more commonly we use acrylic, PVA (polyvinyl acetate) or even plastic sealers which can be either painted or sprayed on, and these are probably most suitable for general use on papers and over paints.

It is very important that you always seal paper before cutting. There are two main reasons for this: one is to strengthen the paper, which makes it easier to cut and minimises tearing; the other is to seal the print and colours on to the paper so they will not come off when the paper gets wet or is touched with a dry or sticky finger!

SHELLAC

Shellac is made from the secretion of the lac insect, and is a sealer and isolator or separator. It comes in various forms and grades, but for découpage only use *white* shellac. A useful sealer for raw wood, it can also be employed to seal your prints although it is a little yellowing. It can also be used to isolate an oil-based product from a water-based product (see Oil and Water page 18).

Work with your brush quickly when applying shellac and don't over-brush — it dries almost immediately. If it becomes too sticky or thick, thin it a little with methylated spirits.

Shellac has a limited shelf life of approximately 12 months.

STAINS

Beautiful effects can be obtained by staining wood as an alternative to painting. In this way you can take advantage of the naturally attractive grains in the wood. It is important, however, that you do *not* seal your wood first as the stain must be able to sink into the timber.

There are a number of different kinds of stains, but for découpage, use ready-made oil-based stains which can be bought in a variety of colours and are probably the easiest to use. Do bear in mind that the colour of the underlying wood will affect the colour of the stain you use. Mahogany under a stain, for instance, will look quite different from raw pine.

Water-based stains have the disadvantage of making the grain of the wood swell and lift. On the positive side, you can make them quite easily yourself. By mixing well either a little artist's acrylic, gouache or writing ink with water and then diluting it by trial and error to the colour you require, you can create a water-based wash. If you wish to deepen the colour, leave each coat to dry well and then brush on a further coat until you get the density you require. You will need to sand well before proceeding as the water draws up the grain of the wood and the surface will have become rough. Seal immediately when dry.

SURFACES

Practically any flat surface is suitable for découpage. Wood, glass, plastic, tin,

So many surfaces and objects can be decorated with découpage. Included amongst the surfaces here are porcelain, bisque, wood, glass, pottery, plastic, silk, mother-of-pearl, shell and stone. Everything from earrings to lampshades, boxes and vases can be made beautiful with découpage.

Other examples of surfaces: soap, stone, wood and even hand-painted eggs.

brass, marble, stone, silk, shells, porcelain, bisque, soap, tiles and walls are all excellent surfaces for decoration. However, be aware that plastic does not react well to turpentine.

VARNISHES

Varnishes can be purchased in mat, satin or gloss finishes.

Water-based varnishes

Découpeurs are luckier these days than in days of yore because water-based varnishes are available. They are easy to use as brushes can be cleaned in water and spills are quick to deal with. Best of all, they dry more quickly than oil-based varnishes (also often referred to as resin varnishes). They are mostly acrylic or PVA based and drying time can vary from 15 minutes to 3 hours — so look at the instructions. They are inclined to be less 'yellowing' than oil-based varnishes, but they create a softer surface and are most suitable for purely decorative objects. Therefore, they are not to be recommended for use on their own on furniture, trays or similar objects that receive wear and tear, in which case always finish with 6 coats of oil-based varnish.

You will find some water-based varnishes have a thicker consistency than others and therefore have a quick build-up in varying degrees.

Oil-based varnishes

Oil-based varnishes are those which require mineral turpentine for clean up. They also have a yellowing effect on your prints and paints and give a more mellow and aged appearance than water-based varnishes. Certain colours such as pinks, mauves and pale blues can be adversely affected under oil-based varnish, and is something learned by trial and error, so take care when using such colours.

Some of these varnishes are more yellowing than others. A useful tip is to take a piece of glass and apply to it about 25 layers of oil-based varnish. You can then place it over your prints and paints and see how the colours are affected.

General advice

Whether to use a satin or gloss varnish is largely a matter of personal choice. A satin finish is probably more suitable if an aged or antique look is required. However, if you are using prints with an oriental flavour and wish to give a real lacquered look, then use gloss. It looks particularly effective over black or chinese reds.

It is important to remember that some varnishes do not sit happily one upon the other, so if you are mixing varnishes check that they are compatible, even if they are both water-based or both are oil-based.

Store tins of oil-based varnish upside down as a skin tends to form after the air has got into it. The skin will therefore be at the bottom of the tin when it is opened.

If your oil-based varnish has developed a skin on it be strong-minded and throw it out — otherwise it will only cause you heartache.

Never shake oil-based varnishes as this creates bubbles which you will find are very hard to get rid of when you are applying the varnish to a surface. It is essential to stir mat varnish very well while gloss varnish can be used undisturbed. However, it is wise to get into the habit of always reading instructions on tins before you start work.

The best way to replace the lid on a tin of varnish, and indeed paint, is to put the tin on the ground and stand on it; that way the lid and rim will not become distorted as can happen if you hammer the lid on.

If your varnishes get a bit lumpy the problem can often be solved by sieving them a couple of times through a nylon stocking.

Always try to varnish in a dust-free environment and do not wear fluffy clothing.

3

Tips and Techniques

Occasionally when you are working on a piece of découpage, you may encounter a problem you have not faced before. I hope these trouble-shooting tips (listed in alphabetical order) will help you to avoid the situation before you get to it — or, if not, help you out of it!

AIR BUBBLES OR LUMPS

If, when you have glued your prints down and they are dry, you discover an air bubble or patch that has not adhered to the surface, make a tiny slit in it at an angle with your scalpel, or prick it with a pin.

Gently ease and push some glue into the slit and under the paper and press down. You will have to use a coloured pencil skilfully to hide the mark of the cut. You can also do this even if you have already applied a few coats of varnish — but it is a bit more tricky since the varnish can split or flake. However, a delicate sand and then more varnish should repair things.

If there are persistent air bubbles which you have been unable to re-move when applying prints under glass, you can release them by tiny pin pricks through the paper.

Likewise, if there is a lump of glue captured under the paper, make a tiny incision and ease it out.

CHIPS OR DENTS

Horrors! If you have chipped or dented your precious découpaged object all is not lost.

Remove the polish (if it has already been applied) with turpentine, then sand round the edge of the chip until the sharp edges have gone. With a small brush carefully drip some var-nish into the chip or dent, letting each drop dry before you apply the next, until you have built up the surface of the chip or dent to the level of the surface. Sand and repolish.

CLEAN AIR

As a dust-free environment is so important for successful découpage, one of the best places to leave a varnished object to dry is in your shower recess, so long as there is no talcum powder about.

It is ideal to spray the air with a fine water spray (used for laundry pur-poses or spraying plants) since this also helps to clear the air of any floating particles.

The art of découpage makes you develop a fine eye for prints and papers. There are so many irresistible pictures and designs available, you are sure to become a 'paper junkie'!

If large objects are being varnished, especially with a gloss finish, it is advisable to rig up a tent above the object with damp sheets. This may be tedious to do, but it will save you time and effort when it comes to sanding!

Small objects may be covered by a box that has plenty of air holes punched in it.

COLLECTING AND STORING PAPER

When transporting paper, roll it, never fold it. Ideally store your paper flat.

Build up a library of cut-outs so you can dip into it when you are planning a project — this can save a lot of time. Keep prints in a labelled concertina file and store cut-outs in plastic envelopes or in photograph albums of the self-adhesive kind.

CRAZED OR WRINKLED VARNISH

This can be a nasty shock! It has probably occurred because the varnish was applied in conditions of high humidity or another coat was added before the previous one was really dry. It is also more inclined to happen if you have applied the varnish too thickly. Be strong minded and leave your creation for at least a week, then dry sand it lightly and continue to varnish. It is bound to be okay after a few more applications!

CUTTING

There are some essential rules to follow when cutting out:

- Work in a good light.
- Use small, fine-bladed scissors, preferably curved.
- Hold both the scissors and the paper lightly and try to relax your shoulders.
- Use your thumb and third or fourth finger in the scissor handle with the first finger under the shank of the scissors to steady them.
- With the blade of your curved scissors turned out (i.e. away from the paper), move the paper around the blades of the scissors — not the scissors around the paper.
- Keep the palm of your cutting hand facing up as you cut; in this way

you will achieve a nice bevelled edge and not a hard straight one.
- Wiggle your paper backwards and forwards very lightly in the blades of the scissors as you cut to give a softer look to the cut edge.

Practise these techniques for a while and you will be very cheered to discover how quickly you improve and how much speedier you become.

There are some other important points to remember:

Do not try to cut out your print holding a large unwieldy piece of paper. With a large pair of scissors quickly cut away most of the excess paper surrounding the print you are using. Next, cut from the inside area first, moving outwards. You will then have a solid bit of paper to hang on to until you have practically finished. If you cut the outside area first, you may find you have to hold on to something delicate, such as the branch of a tree, while you are cutting the inner portions of the print.

It is also important to leave joining ladders or branches from one delicate portion to another, for example from the stem of one flower to another. This lessens the chance of the stems being damaged by your fingers while you are cutting out the surrounding area. So look at your print and draw in the ladders before you start. When you have finished, just snip the ladders off. If you have some small internal surrounding areas that need to be removed, and you wish to use your scissors rather than a scalpel, cut a small slit into the middle of that area with the point of your blade. Then come up from underneath with the scissors and cut so that the paper can be moved easily around the top of your blades.

A scalpel or craft knife may be used to cut out delicate or very small areas. This should ideally be done on a firm piece of cardboard or better still on a special cutting mat designed for the purpose and found in art or graphic design stores. Keep the scalpel blade at a slight angle sloping away from the paper. Use of the scalpel should be kept to a minimum as you cannot achieve the same soft and bevelled edges that you can with scissors.

DRYING GLASS

The most satisfactory way to dry recently washed glass is with tissue paper — that way you will not have to deal with lint and fluff.

DRYING OBJECTS

To dry a painted or varnished object, invert it over a small jar or bottle. Put a little Blu-Tack on the lid of the jar or bottle to keep the object firmly attached. A revolving object like a Lazy Susan cake stand is also a very useful tool to use when varnishing an object.

If you are drying a decorated egg, put a thin knitting needle through the hole through which it has been blown and stand it in a florist's sponge.

GLOSS FINISHES

If you are having difficulty creating a clean, smooth gloss finish, use a rolled-up stocking with a piece of cotton wadding in it, dip it lightly in the gloss varnish and firmly wipe the surface. Do this two or three times. This is especially useful for gloss varnish but works on a satin finish as well.

Another method is to thin your gloss varnish down with turpentine (about 1 part turps to 2 parts varnish) and paint a thin coat over the imperfect surface.

MAKING A TACK CLOTH

Sometimes tack cloths are hard to track down (they are used by the automotive industry, and can also be found in some large hardware stores, paint shops and good craft supply shops), but you can make your own quite easily.

Soak some clean cheesecloth or loosely woven, lint-free cotton material (about 15 cm/6 in square) in warm water and wring it out well.

Damp the cloth thoroughly with mineral turpentine but don't soak it. Now sprinkle a tablespoon of oil-based varnish over it and squeeze it well so that the varnish is absorbed throughout the cloth. The cloth should not be wet but just slightly sticky so that it picks up the dust but does not dampen a surface as you wipe it.

It is important that a tack cloth does not dry out, so do not leave it lying around, but be sure to keep it stored in an airtight jar. It can have a long life as long as it does not get too dry or dirty. A few drops of water and varnish and further kneading from time to time will ensure it remains usable.

MILKY BLOOM ON VARNISH

This is also believed to be caused by dampness — humidity or, dare I say it, a little impatience or haste? It may also have something to do with the quality of the varnish.

Try sanding it off, it may work. If not I am afraid you just have to live with it or give it to the white elephant stall.

PAINTED BACKGROUNDS

You can have great fun experimenting with painted backgrounds. Here are some simple ideas.

Paint your background, then, choosing a portion of a natural sea sponge with the most holes, dip that area into a contrasting coloured paint. Blot off the excess on some paper and then lightly dab the sponge on your painted surface.

Alternatively, paint your background, and when dry, once again choose a strongly contrasting colour and paint it over the first colour. When the second coat is thoroughly dry, take a medium-grade sandpaper and gently sand random streaky patches until the colour underneath comes through. This will give a worn effect to the surface. Give the edges and corners a particularly good sand since those are the areas that tend to receive wear and tear. This effect is called 'distressing'.

To achieve a spatter finish on a pre-painted surface, dilute some paint with water. Dip a toothbrush in it and then run your thumb along the bristles so that a spray or spatter of paint falls lightly on the surface.

Antiquing is an interesting way of making an object look old. You can buy ready-made antiquing finishes, in which case just read the instructions about how to use them. Alternatively you can make a wash with your paint by adding water and then sponge or paint it on to your surface. Wipe the dilution off fairly quickly with a dry cloth so that only a subtle coating of colour is left behind. Raw umber is a suitable colour for this purpose but you can use others of your choice — just experiment. Leave some of the colour sitting in grooves and corners so that it looks like the grime of years.

PICKING UP PRINTS

Apart from using your fingers or tweezers, a nifty way of picking up small prints is to put a blob of Blu-Tack on the end of a toothpick and then prod the print with the Blu-Tack. The print will adhere easily and will also be easy to disengage. This method works just as successfully with dry prints as when gluing and positioning prints.

POLISHING

There are various methods of polishing. A simple but effective way is to polish with toothpaste and a soft damp cloth.

Two other well-tried and tested materials are pumice and rottenstone. If you have used an oil-based varnish, use either of these two materials in conjunction with a felt/cloth wad, which has been well soaked in raw linseed oil or olive oil (the former is preferable).

If you have used a water-based varnish, combine the pumice or rottenstone with a water-soaked cloth. These materials both give a wonderful finish.

For final polishing, always use a good quality wax. The best is beeswax, preferably combined with carnauba wax but certainly without silicone. Apply with a damp cloth, leave for a few minutes and polish with a soft cloth. Do not use spray polishes — they are too drying. Polish frequently.

One of the best ways to develop a beautiful patina on your piece of découpage is to pick it up regularly and polish it with the palms of your hands as the natural oil from your skin gives it a wonderful lustre. This could be difficult if your object is a chest of drawers!

PRE-VARNISHED AND PRE-PAINTED OBJECTS

If you want to découpage an object that has already been varnished or painted, and you would like to use that existing surface, be sure to remove all grease and dirt by washing the surface well with detergent and water and drying it thoroughly. If there are stubborn dirty and greasy patches, use methylated spirits. You do not need to seal the surface because the original varnish or paint has sealed it already.

If, on the other hand, you prefer to strip the object back to the raw wood, you can use a commercially prepared stripper if sanding it back by hand is too big an operation. Remember, though, if you expose the raw wood, it must be sealed again before you begin working on the surface.

As far as possible, always remove fittings such as hinges and handles because trying to varnish with fittings in place is filled with pitfalls. The only time it is wise to leave them in place is if you are preparing an antique and the fittings are old and delicate. In this case trying to remove them may damage them and even render them useless.

PROTECTION OF BRUSHES

Synthetic brushes used for gesso or water-based paints and varnishes should be washed well in detergent and water and then thoroughly rinsed.

Brushes used for oil-based paints and varnishes are cleaned in mineral turpentine. To save time when you are using an oil-based varnish, fill two jars with mineral turpentine. Rinse the brush around thoroughly in one and leave it suspended in the other. You can do this by holding it across the top of the jar with a peg or suspend it through the teat of a baby's bottle. (However, as the fumes of turpentine are toxic, it is healthier to keep a lid on your jar — pierce a hole in the lid through which to put your brush handle.) At all times be careful not to let the bristles rest on the bottom of the jar or they will become misshapen. Make sure you keep the turpentine clean, particularly the second bottle in which the brush is hanging. The moment it gets cloudy or solid bits in it — chuck it out!

Alternatively, having rinsed your brush well, you should wrap it firmly in foil, making sure it is airtight. This helps to keep the brush's shape.

If you are not going to be using your brush for some time, clean it well in mineral turpentine, then with soap and water, rinse thoroughly and leave to dry. It is not good to rinse natural bristle brushes in detergent as it destroys the natural oils in the hair. It is best to use a proper brush cleaner or just soap and water.

Brushes used for shellac should be cleaned in methylated spirits, so be careful not to put them inadvertently in turpentine or they will be rendered useless!

There are some good brush cleaners on the market; try a crafts shop or hardware store. They certainly help prolong the life of your brushes.

It is important to always keep separate brushes for paint and varnish as dried fragments of one can get into the other and cause you problems as they transfer themselves to the surface when you paint or varnish.

RUST

Old tin objects often lend themselves beautifully to being découpaged. However, it is essential that you remove any existing rust and prevent further rust. Firstly, sand the surface hard to remove any rust that may be present and then paint it well all over with a rust inhibitor before painting and decorating.

SANDING

It is easier and more satisfactory to use a sanding block around which to wrap your sandpaper when sanding flat surfaces — you get a more even finish.

Be sure to seal wood before wet sanding, otherwise the water may warp the wood or the damp may remain captured in the wood and show itself later as some horrendous problem! The wood can rot, the paint can lift and the varnish can crack or peel off.

Try not to sand in the same room as you varnish. The dust will not improve the quality of your varnish!

SANDING THROUGH THE VARNISH

This has to be one of the most common disasters for beginners, and one of the most traumatic, but really it generally isn't all that serious, so relax.

If you have sanded through to your print and removed some of the colour, select coloured pencils to match the print (a touch darker than the original colour), dip them in some turpentine and smoothly blend in the colours over the rubbed area. You can do a similar repair by cautiously painting the area with very thin acrylic paint. Seal before re-varnishing. If you carry out either of these steps carefully, I guarantee no one would ever know!

If you have sanded back to the wood, dab a little of the original paint on to the offending spot, then rub in the colour with your finger. When the area is well covered, put some sealer over the paint and continue to varnish. The only time you can face a real problem with this repair technique is if you have mixed your own colour and it is difficult to match. For this reason it is wise always to keep aside a little of any mixed paint for such contingencies.

Just remember next time not to be so heavy-handed with the sanding and take particular care not to sand the sharp edges and corners too much — they are always a danger spot.

SCISSORS

Never keep your scissors in the plastic cover in which they are often sold because it causes sweating and rusts them. Be sure to oil the hinges of your scissors from time to time and protect the points by placing them in a cork when not in use. Never use your découpage scissors for any purpose other than for cutting thin paper and never lend them to anybody. They should be treated as a precious precision instrument!

SUPPORT FOR A HINGED BOX

It is wise to support the lid of a hinged box (other than very small ones) with a chain or ribbon so that the lid does not fall too far back and cause strain on the hinges. This should be done by attaching one end of the ribbon or chain to the lid and the other to the box at a position of 'a quarter past three' from the hinges (at 'twelve o'clock'). This causes the support to fall *into* the box, not out, as you close the lid. Slip the ends under the lining of the side of the lid and the side of the box respectively. If the box is not lined, then glue the support to this position and stick something decorative over the ends.

THINNING PAPER

Don't discard any cards or calendar prints that appear too thick to use — often you can peel them carefully to make them thinner.

Paint a coat of sealer on the back of the print and, when dry, with your fingernails split the paper layers at a corner and gently pull them apart. As they separate roll the excess layer around a pencil or knitting needle. Very gently sand the rough paper at the back of the print with a fine sandpaper and apply a layer of sealer.

If the paper is very thick, you can sand the back with a coarse sandpaper and then smooth with fine sandpaper. This is fraught with danger, so be careful!

If the paper is not thick enough to split, but is too thick to be practical to use, then it is best to treat it like a transfer (also known as a decal). There are a number of materials sold for the purpose of making decals but you can also use a water-based sealer or varnish. (Liquitex Gloss Medium and Varnish is ideal for this.) Paint the *face* of the print with at least six layers of the sealer/varnish, allowing each coat to dry well. Then place the print in tepid water and leave to soak for at least two hours. Take it out (it normally curls up in the water), put it down on a piece of waxed paper on a firm surface and gently rub off the wet paper from the back of the picture with your finger, being careful not to rub a hole. Keep your finger wet. Eventually there will appear a very thin film keeping the picture intact. When it is dry, very gingerly sand with fine sandpaper to smooth and then seal the back and cut in the normal way.

TORN PAPER

To repair a piece of torn paper, paint a thin layer of an adhesive varnish or white glue on to the back of the tear and stick on a patch of tissue or rice paper. Sometimes it may be necessary to make good the front of the tear with your coloured pencils.

TOXINS

It is always wise to remember that the fumes of methylated spirits, mineral turpentine, oil-based varnishes and sprays are all very toxic if inhaled regularly. It is therefore very important that you always use them in a well-ventilated area.

As well, the fine dust caused by sanding can cause problems for people who suffer from allergies or lung troubles. For this reason, these people should wear a protective mask, even if it is only a simple one. Masks are available from most hardware stores and good craft suppliers.

WATER MARKS OR MOIRÉ

It is very distressing if, when you come to your final sandings, the surface is suddenly covered with lots of squiggly shiny lines — like moiré silk or water taffeta!

No one is sure what causes this, but one theory is that it is the result of atmospheric moisture captured in the varnish. Perhaps the air was humid or damp when you were applying the varnish, or you may just have been too impatient and applied another coat before the previous one was really dry.

The appearance of these lines could also be due to uneven sanding early on. They can often be rubbed away with a dry 0000 wire/steel wool. However, if they are persistent you should revarnish with 3 to 5 coats — or more — and then re-sand.

Sometimes you can get away with wiping on a couple more thin coats of varnish (of whichever kind you are using) with a wad of nylon stocking (see Gloss Finishes page 25) to hide the offenders. Then polish in the normal way.

— 4 —
Design

If people have the artistic and creative desire and ability to practise découpage, they will generally have some innate feeling for design. They may need a little technical advice and a few ideas to produce a pleasing and satisfactory composition, but instinctively they will have a feeling of what looks right and what doesn't.

It is interesting that the concept of 'design' in its modern sense was essentially a nineteenth-century English phenomenon — a by-product of the English industrial revolution. In the mid-nineteenth century a training institution was set up by the Royal College of Art, and encouraged and supported by the Prince Consort and Queen Victoria, to train artists in design for textiles, ceramics and other disciplines. It was not until the nineteenth century that the study of applied ornaments (in which additional ornamentation is added to a structure or surface) and their rich history from early classical and even primitive times was first regarded seriously.

Today we are constantly made aware of design — in the materials of the clothes we wear, the textiles with which we decorate our houses, the shape of buildings, the form of cars and much more, so that consciously and unconsciously we are noting, absorbing and criticising design we see all round us. In addition, everyone uses design on a daily basis. Colour, shape and design play a part when a woman chooses her make-up and hair style. The principles of design come to the fore when we select and wear jewellery. We are designing when we arrange flowers in a bowl or decorate a cake. Design influences the way we place the furniture in our houses or plan the layout of a garden.

Design is a huge and complex subject, but here we will simply consider some basic concepts that anyone can put into practice.

To begin with, we tend to undertake a découpage project in one of two ways. We may first decide upon a specific object, a tray, a coffee table, a chest of drawers, a thimble or a pair of earrings. If the object is your first choice, then you have probably already decided what the predominant colour will be. If it is a coffee table you will want it to match or blend in with your general furnishing colours. In the same manner, you will choose a colour for your earrings to match the clothes in your wardrobe. Next there is the challenge of finding the appropriate prints with which to decorate your object — something modern, Baroque, chinoiserie, flowers or figures: the choice is endless. But stop — does your choice of prints suit the object to be decorated? Would you put Victorian prints on a Georgian knife box? Presumably not. So you must search for prints that enhance and complement your object. Then you must decide whether they suit and are enhanced by the background colour.

There is another way of tackling the challenge. You may have found some stunning wrapping paper or a book with illustrations you adore and which you just have to use for a découpage project. In this case you are governed by the prints. What colour can you pick out of the prints as a background or what contrasting colour would make the most of them? Having decided on that, you must consider what object would best display and suit

Screen, walking sticks, box and egg. Découpage under varnish on a variety of objects and using pre-coloured prints. Created by Lola McNickle.

your prints. Think of shape. You would not normally put elongated designs such as statues on a round box whereas they might be more suitable for a tall lamp base.

So now you are about to design and compose your own creations. Observe the world around you and notice how the elements of form, shape, position, colour and size compose themselves. Study paintings, textiles, ceramics and decorator items to get a feel of design. Analyse why one thing pleases and another doesn't.

COLOUR

Colour is an integral part of design. It should always be considered because it plays a part in the general character of the work you are planning.

Consideration of colour is based on the way different colours, shades and tones work together, and some understanding of the way colours relate to each other on the colour wheel is useful. For information on colour and palettes see *Hand Colouring* page 64.

While it is not essential to be overly theoretical about the use of colour — instinct and personal taste play a large part in your choice of colours — it is wise to remember that certain combinations can be inappropriate. For example, if you are decorating an antique, you would not normally select bright, stark modern colours. On the other hand, such colours are wonderful when used on a child's toy chest.

When selecting a melange of prints to go together on an object, remember that as well as being stylistically compatible, they should also exhibit compatible colouring. For example, do not mix too many different reds — although they are all 'red', the different shades may 'scream' at each other.

POSITIONING YOUR CUT-OUTS

There is a tendency in many of us to favour symmetry, and while that may be safe and mildly pleasing, it doesn't generally set the world on fire, and can often be just plain dull! An exception are textile designs such as those of William Morris, or art deco patterns, which are more often than not symmetrical and repetitive with pleasing results. Art and design have gone through many changes of style such as the periods of Classicism (order and symmetry) and Romanticism (freedom of line and design, and 'disorder'). Neoclassicism and Art Deco is ordered and structured, while Art Nouveau is free and flowing.

Try to create contrast or 'tension'. Establish a focal point to which the rest of your design is led. The focal point may be obvious when it is, for instance, the largest print in your composition, or the one with most appeal. It may be where the eye is led by movement, position or even colour. Having decided on the focal point, most of the other prints should complement and relate to it.

If you place two figures on the lid of a box, position them so that they face each other. In this way your eyes will be drawn to where the figures are looking. If that is not possible, arrange the figures so that they both gaze in

Hand-coloured prints on silk showing the principal motif positioned to one side with the figures moving in the same direction, thus drawing the eye with them. Created by a member of the National Guild of Découpeurs (USA).

the same direction; this will lead your eyes automatically that way. Do not put two figures back to back so that your eyes are led in opposite directions, reducing the impact of the design.

If, for example, you use butterflies, try to place them so they fly towards the same focal point — if they move in different directions, it can be visually exhausting!

When designing a running or continuous pattern (such as garlands of flowers) to decorate the side of a box, or the perimeter of a tray, try to emulate the shape of a figure 'S' flowing horizontally — it gives a pleasing continuity to your design.

Proportion is important — the proportion of your prints to the article you are decorating and the prints in relation to each other. A large print should not dominate the object it decorates, but relate sympathetically while enhancing it.

As a general rule (although there are exceptions), do not place your principal print right in the middle of the box — or whatever surface you are decorating. Place it a little to one side and accompany it with prints of a contrasting size which are subordinate to it. This will give your composition balance. Be careful if you plan to place most of your prints on one side and leave the opposite side undecorated as this will probably create a top heavy appearance. Even a small addition in a bare area can make all the difference.

Which of the following is the most interesting:

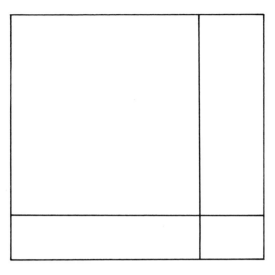

B

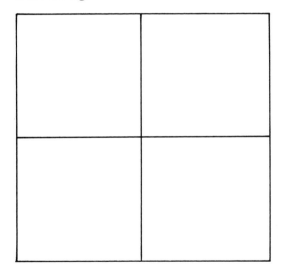

A

I'm sure you will say 'B'. Why? Because it is asymmetrical and does not have the centre as its focal point.

Do remember that if you place a print across the base and the lid of a box, you will have to slice it to open the box. therefore make sure to position the print so that you don't have to cut through the face or head of a person or animal. Aim to cut through a hat, or through the lower neck or shoulders.

SELECTING PRINTS

When selecting your prints, choose illustrations and designs that are compatible and relate to each other in style, subject, colour and form. Do not, for example, mix Victorian scraps with Japanese wood blocks as they are too different in nature. Likewise modern stark flower drawings with detailed antique Flemish flower paintings.

Don't combine strongly coloured bold prints with soft pastel ones because they will overpower them. Remember, you are the artist at work decorating an object, so you would not mix your styles and strengths of colour — your work would be uniform. Of course one should be free to be creative and in modern day découpage anything goes — but this book is specifically about traditional découpage. I am not saying do not use modern prints — indeed, they can look stunning — I just do not advocate a mélange of different styles and disconnected objects for a piece of classical découpage. But if you want to be a Salvador Dali with a clock here and an eye there, go for it!

PERSPECTIVE

This should be considered as well. Remember, an object nearest to you is larger than one in the distance. It is also darker, because things look fainter in the distance.

So for the sake of perspective place bigger prints at the front and smaller prints to the side and back.

Relate the size of one object to another and be realistic. Do not have a rose beside a huge butterfly that dwarfs it, or a child next to a cat twice its size. This is a common error and can detract from an otherwise artistic composition.

MORE OR LESS?

People differ in their views as to how fully or sparsely they may like to decorate an object. That is a matter of personal taste, but, in general, discretion is the better part of valour and too little is probably preferable to too much. If in doubt — *stop*.

Space is as important as the prints used: it complements and distinguishes the design. So give as much thought to the space you will have as to the prints chosen.

Simplicity is the key to elegance; however if you are decorating in the Victorian style or creating a fun toy chest for a child it would be appropriate to cover your surface lavishly.

Take time over the design. Use Blu-Tack to place your prints in varying positions until you are satisfied. Stand back, take a walk around the room and then come back and take a final look at your efforts before taking the irrevocable step of gluing them down.

One last bit of advice: don't get so keen on a particular print, even if it is your main one, that you cannot discard it. If it is not working, put it aside — there are plenty more fish in the sea! It is so easy to waste hours trying to create a composition or to combine other prints with one or two you particularly want to use. It may not work out. Recognise the fact and start again. Often by discarding a troublesome print or two, the design will suddenly come together.

Design is a major part of your creativity, so do not be inhibited; follow your taste and instincts.

5

Basic Découpage Under Varnish

Découpage under varnish is the most traditional execution of this art form, and a small wooden box is an excellent object to use for a first project. In addition, timber is an admirable surface for découpage. The photographs in this chapter show the use of prints from a calendar and the cut-outs have been applied to a warm white background.

Before starting the following project, read the chapter *Materials — Information and Uses* in order to understand the instructions. Likewise, study the chapter *Tips and Techniques*, it could save you a heart attack.

MATERIALS

The following materials are the basic requirements needed for most découpage projects, so you should always have them on hand:

A good selection of wrapping papers, cards, calendars, prints
A suitable object to decorate (in this case a simple craftwood box, preferably with smooth straight sides)
Timber putty or wood filler
Two soft flat-edged paint brushes ¾"
or 1" (2 or 2.5 cm) (one synthetic; one natural bristle)
Sponge brush (Polybrush)
Very small fine brush, 000 or 0000 in size
A rubber brayer (roller)
Acrylic gesso
Sealer
Blu-Tack
PVA glue
Small sea-sponge
Small fine-bladed scissors — preferably curved cuticle scissors
Scalpel or craft knife
Ordinary scissors for general use
Tack cloth (for removing dust — see page 25) found in auto shops, some hardware or paint shops, and some craft suppliers
Cutting mat or thick cardboard
Waxed kitchen paper
Wet-and-dry sandpaper Nos 400, 600 and 1000/1200
0000 steel wool
Coloured pencils (not watercolour)
Acrylic paints
Toothpick
Mineral turpentine
Sanding sealer (optional)
Oil and/or water-based varnishes
Car-cutting compound (optional)
Good quality wax furniture polish (preferably without silicone and ideally with carnauba wax)

Pre-coloured prints of Erté's alphabet theatrical costumes. 'W' by Audrey Raymond.

DECOUPAGE ON A WOOD BOX

TECHNIQUE

Note: If the box has hinges, remove them carefully and set aside.

SANDING

Sand the box lightly with 400 wet-and-dry sandpaper used dry. If the size of the surface warrants it, use a felt-backed sanding block, folding the sandpaper around it. (With a sanding block you can achieve an even surface with less effort!) If you are working with a grained wood, sand in the same direction as the grain of the wood. Don't go across the grain as you may tear it. Fill in any holes or imperfections with the wood filler, used sparingly to prevent excessive sanding later. Some fillers shrink a little as they dry, so don't be *too* sparing with the application. When no longer damp, dry sand with 400 wet-and-dry sandpaper until the filler is absolutely smooth and flat against the surface.

If bits of glue from making the box are protruding, remove them with a chisel or craft knife. If they are persistent, try heating a knife and holding it against the glue to melt it.

Remember to keep wiping your box with the tack cloth to remove all dust after sanding.

From now on get into the habit of picking up your tack cloth and wiping your box before every stage of the operation — sanding, painting and varnishing. It is so important to keep the surface you are working on clean. Flies, hairs, fluff and foreign bodies of a fascinating variety love to lie in wait to catch you unawares when you are applying the next coat of paint or varnish!

SEALING

Now the surface must be sealed. There are two alternatives.

The first is to seal the wood all over with a suitable sealer. If you are only going to do that, your surface must be very well sanded to make sure there are no obvious thick wood grains or little dents, otherwise they will show through your painted finish.

The second and better alternative, is to coat the surface with a minimum of six coats of gesso using your sponge brush. Dry sand very lightly between coats and wet sand the final coat. Then put aside for 48 hours to dry and cure. (See Gesso on page 16.) When dry, use your tack cloth!

PAINTING

When the surface is dry, the next step is to paint it. Remember that it is important to take care when you are painting and varnishing (now and later) not to fill in the holes where the hinges go. A good idea is to stick a toothpick into the holes to avoid that danger.

Choose a background colour which will enhance your prints; do not just choose a colour because it is one of your favourites. If you are having difficulty deciding, bear in mind that many prints look wonderful on a black background or on warm white. As a guideline, select one of the darker colours in your prints as background colour or look at the palest colours and choose one of those. However, be careful: if the print is in soft tones, make sure the end result doesn't look insipid.

You can either buy the background colour ready mixed or mix your own. If you decide to mix your own colours, do be sure to make enough to cover your whole box in one go because it is very difficult to mix the exact colour again just to complete a small area.

Before you begin painting always dampen your brush first in water or turpentine, whichever is the appropriate medium for the paint you are using. Be sure it is only damp, *not* wet.

Apply each coat (and this goes for gesso and varnish too), in the opposite direction to the previous coat, that is, at right angles.

Apply at least 3 coats of acrylic paint, sanding very lightly between coats but not after the final coat. You need to have a good solid depth of colour. (Remember that tack cloth!) If your paint is uneven or shows brush marks you could be putting it on too thickly, or the paint may be too thick. If you are using acrylics add a tiny bit of water to the paint, or in the case of oil paint, a small amount of mineral turpentine.

Next, apply a coat of sealer all over your painted surfaces.

Finally, always remember to wash out your brushes immediately after using them. Do not leave them to harden with whatever material you have been using — you will ruin them and it becomes expensive. (See Protection of Brushes on page 27.)

INSIDE THE BOX

Let's stop a moment to talk about the inside of your box. It should be sealed with a wood sealer. If you are going to line it, paint down about 2 cm inside from the top edges. I say, 'If you are going to line it', because it seems a pity to go to the trouble of making an exquisite box on the outside and then not bother making it equally beautiful with a rich lining inside. So often one sees a wonderful box and it is such a let down to find it is just painted inside and often not all that well. However, if I have not convinced you, then make sure you have sanded the interior thoroughly before sealing it, or better still, put some coats of gesso inside so that at least you have a good-looking painted surface within.

CHOOSING YOUR PRINTS

Select your prints by choosing designs that are of a similar style and tonal colouring, and preferably those with well-defined outlines.

Never mix pre-coloured prints with hand-coloured ones. Remember the box is supposed to be the work of one artist.

Choose well-executed drawings and paintings on good quality paper and be very wary of using magazine pictures with newsprint on the back because this often bleeds through when you glue the print down. Spray or paint the print with a sealer on the front and look carefully to see if the newsprint shows through; also hold the paper up to the light and if you can see the newsprint it is generally wiser to be strong-minded and cast it into the wastepaper basket.

Paintings or drawings are usually preferable to photographs as the outlines in photographs are not always well defined and there can be a lack of light and shade which is necessary to give a defined shape or feeling of depth.

Look carefully at the print to see if there are any very fine lines such as stems, twigs, butterflies' antennae, beaks of birds and the like, which can be difficult to cut out. If so, you should cheat here by using a coloured pencil of an appropriate colour to thicken the lines and so make cutting out easier.

Paint 2 thin coats of sealer over the *face* of the prints before you start to cut them out. This prevents the paper tearing as you cut and it also seals the colour of the print to stop it fading or running later when it is damp. *This is a very important step.* (See Sealers on page 18.)

CUTTING OUT

Fine cutting is one of the most important parts of découpage and requires practice. However, you can become adept quite quickly and it is very enjoyable, engrossing and therapeutic. Besides, it is pleasing to be able to bask in paeans of praise as people admire your skill with scissors.

Before you begin cutting out your prints for your first project, read the section in *Tips and Techniques* on page

Once you have prepared the surface to be découpaged and have selected your prints, seal the prints and then *carefully cut them out.*

24. Remember, however, there are some essential rules to follow: work in a good light and use small, fine-bladed scissors, preferably curved.

A scalpel may be used to cut out delicate or very small areas (see page 25). However, use of the scalpel should be kept to a minimum as you cannot achieve the same soft and bevelled edges that you can with scissors.

PAINTING THE EDGES

Now here comes the only boring bit. Although painting edges to disguise the white of the paper is a rather tedious process it is a *must* for a professional looking piece of découpage. It gives your cut-out a much tidier and defined outline and

To stop the cut edges of the prints showing as a hard white line, *carefully paint along the edges being careful not to get paint on the face of your print.* Choose a colour that blends with the colours in your prints — but *not* white.

hides any little imperfections in your cutting. Once you have done it, you will see what a difference it makes! Besides, like cutting, with a bit of practice you will learn to whiz along.

With a tiny 0000 brush, paint the cut white edges of paper with acrylic paint, using colours that co-ordinate with the print.

Hold the cut-out at right angles to your body and roll the brush along the cut white edge making sure that no paint gets on to the face of the print. This is best done by holding the brush so that it points to the back of the print — in other words the face of the print is away from the brush.

Keep checking that no paint is getting on to the face of your print. If it does, remove it immediately with a damp sponge or your fingers — take great care about this.

Don't use black to outline edges, it is too strong and hard, use dark brown or umber shade for the darkest areas. Likewise do not ever paint edges white or a very light colour as it is pointless and does not give the distinct tidy line you are trying to achieve. About the only exception to this rule is when you are doing the profile of a face.

Rather than using paint, you may wish to hold the print down and run a coloured pencil (preferably dipped in turpentine) along the cut edge, but this method is not necessarily as effective, because you do not get such good coverage, nor is it much easier or quicker.

DESIGNING YOUR COMPOSITION

Having read the section on *Design* page 31 you should now start moving your cut-outs around the box until you have a composition that pleases you.

Place the cut-outs temporarily in position with a small piece of Blu-Tack under each one. You can use tweezers for moving tiny or delicate prints.

Alternatively, until you become more experienced it is sometimes easier to make a paper template of the surfaces of the box and move the prints around on that until you are happy with your design.

Fine-tune your design by arranging the prints on the surface you wish to decorate. Use Blu-Tack to attach the prints. Note that prints can extend over the join of the box and its lid. They can be sliced through later.

GLUING

Always work on a piece of waxed paper so prints won't stick down when being glued. Dispense a quantity of glue into a dish and then one by one lift each print, remove the Blu-Tack and apply the glue to the underside of the print. Make sure you cover the whole surface well, extending the glue to the edges.

It is important to keep your finger-tips moistened with water while sticking down your prints otherwise they will stick to you. It is useful to have a pair of tweezers on hand with which to pick up and place down your prints. Position the print and pat down firmly with a well wrung-out sponge.

When gluing very delicate or tiny prints, it is easier to apply the glue to the painted surface and then place the cut-out down on to it. Massage the glue well into the surface. This exercise will require more careful cleaning up of the surface afterwards.

If you are gluing fairly large prints, it is best to use a roller (brayer) to ensure that the glue is spread evenly, that there are no lumps left behind and the print is flat and well stuck down. Also this will remove excess glue. Place a piece of wax paper over the print, or a damp cloth or piece of damp kitchen towel, before gently rolling the brayer over your print.

After you have finished gluing down the prints, clean off all excess glue with your sponge and leave to dry for 12 hours.

By using a toothpick and holding it nearly parallel to the surface you are decorating, carefully prod all edges to see if you can lift them. If you can, then they are not stuck down. Additionally, if you hold the surface up to eye level you can see if any tiny bits of paper have not adhered. If this is the case, secure them with a further amount of glue applied with the toothpick.

It does not matter if you wish to place a print over the join of the lid and the base of the box — this can be cut later. However, be sure to put a tiny flat piece of Blu-Tack between the lid and the base to keep them firmly in place, but make sure the Blu-Tack does not make a space between them. If you are working on a hinged box, be sure to put the two hinged sides together. This is sometimes forgotten.

When all the prints have been glued in position take your scalpel or craft knife and slice the paper along the join of the lid and the base. Remember to paint the cut edge and make sure it is well stuck down. Warning! Be prepared for the fact that some glue may have seeped in between the crack of the lid and base of the box so that when you have sliced the print and opened the box it may have stuck and you will therefore have removed a bit of paint. Don't worry — just add a bit of paint to repair it and then seal again.

VARNISHING

Until now your box will be looking like the ugly duckling, but the moment you start applying the water-based varnish it will take on an exciting new look.

With a large, soft synthetic brush or sponge brush (always slightly dampened in water first) start applying a coat of water-based varnish over the box. Let it flow on smoothly but take great care to remove any drips.

Apply the varnish evenly and lightly. Do not overwork or keep brushing in the one spot — try and apply the varnish with long smooth strokes. A number of thin coats is better than fewer thick coats. As with painting, brush each coat on in the opposite direction to the previous coat. If you get a foreign body in the varnish before the tenth coat, just try gently to remove it with a little bit of sandpaper.

Leave to dry for a minimum of 3 hours, or as advised on the container of varnish, in a *dust-free* area. Remember, if there is a lot of humidity in the air it will need double the amount of time to dry. Ideally you

Once the prints have been glued to the surface, 'sink' the print with many carefully applied coats of varnish. Allow each coat to dry thoroughly and after the first 15 coats (and then after every succeeding 5 coats) lightly wet-sand the work to produce a very smooth finish.

should not varnish in a damp or humid atmosphere as it can lead to problems (see pages 24 and 26) — and panic!

If you decide to use an oil-based varnish you should ideally leave 24 hours between coats, again remembering to double that time if the weather is humid. Use a soft, flat natural bristle brush. Apply the varnish in the same way as above but dip your brush in turpentine first. While applying the varnish, be careful not to overwork it or you will leave brush marks.

Do not overload the brush with varnish and do not be tempted to wipe it on the side of the tin — you'll get a build up if you do and you won't be able to close the lid. Just immerse up to half the brush in the varnish and give it a shake so that any excess drops off.

Apply at least 15 coats of varnish before sanding for the first time and more if your print is on thicker-than-average paper. Be careful to sand very gently so as not to rub through to the print and cause damage.

Then, using your 400 wet-and-dry sandpaper saturated in water (to which a little detergent has been added so that you can make suds) *very gently* sand the surface mostly using the suds and taking great care not to be so heavy-handed that you sand away your print! Remove any ridges, drips or dust particles in this way.

Continue applying further coats of varnish. Wet sand as above after every 5 coats, but from now use 600 wet-and-dry.

After 25 to 30 coats of varnish you should not be able to feel your print if you run your finger over the surface — it should be 'sunk'. The number of coats necessary to achieve this beautifully smooth finish will depend greatly on the thickness of your prints and whether or not you overlapped any cut-outs. Be warned — any time you overlap prints on the surface means you will need at least an additional 6 coats of varnish.

Remember not to apply your varnish too thickly and keep checking that there are no drips. If any ridges or drips do form, just wet sand them away gently.

If you are using a water-based varnish to decorate an object that is likely to receive some wear and tear, it is advisable to add at least 6 coats of an oil-based varnish to give a tougher finish. More importantly, if the object is to incur considerable wear and tear — such as a tray or table — you should only ever varnish with an oil-based varnish. This is applied in the same way as water-based varnish except that it is not advisable to use a sponge brush with mineral turpentine, which is used in conjunction with an oil-based varnish. Rather, use a flat, natural bristle brush.

Oil-based sanding sealer (a ready-made product available at hardware stores) is pleasing to use because it builds up quickly, is easy to sand, and gives a beautiful finish. It also fills in little imperfections. But it should *not* be used for final coats since it is too soft.

Also bear in mind that it takes about three months for varnish to 'cure' and harden. During that time be careful not to leave your work wrapped up as it may discolour and the material in which it is wrapped may leave an imprint in the varnish.

Remember to clean your brushes well after every use to ensure their long life.

CUTTING BACK AND POLISHING

When you are finally satisfied that you cannot feel or see any ridges of paper, give all the surfaces a sound sanding with the 1000 or 1200 wet-and-dry paper, well saturated in sudsy water.

Keep sanding until all surfaces are completely dull and you cannot see any shiny spots. It is really important that your box looks absolutely dull because shiny spots represent minute dips in the varnish, which will show up when the finished surface is polished. So at this stage you are cutting back the varnish on your prints to bring it to the level of the varnish on your

The finished box showing découpage under varnish.

background. At the same time you will be levelling and smoothing the complete surface. Don't be dismayed if it looks horrid — that's par for the course!

Rub the surface with the 0000 wire wool to create a perfectly smooth, silky finish. Do not rub in a circular motion but backwards and forwards in one direction and then at right angles in a cross-hatching fashion. You may, if you wish, also use a car-cutting compound or even toothpaste for an even smoother and silkier surface.

You can never polish too much as every technique you use will enhance the finish. If the wire wool makes any tiny scratches, give the surface one more wet sand with the fine 1200 wet-and-dry sandpaper.

When the surface is dry, polish and buff with a good quality furniture polish until you have a glorious lustrous sheen (see *Tips* on polishing page 27). Keep it well polished in the future and the finish will improve with every application. Enjoy touching your découpage creation: for in addition to its visual beauty, its wonderful tactile quality is enhanced by the natural oil in your hands, which gives a lustrous patina to the work.

Now replace the hinges.

The above methods are basic steps of well-executed découpage and you can now apply these techniques to something as small as a thimble or as large as a piece of furniture.

The basic technique of découpage under varnish can be used to decorate many objects. Among them are (from back) the top of a folding table, an octagonal box, two smaller boxes, a hand-held mirror, a crackle-finish box with real insect wings, a small box with gold braid, and wooden earrings.

LINING THIS BOX

Materials needed

Suitable material, such as velvet, satin, brocade

Tacky glue or non-staining, quick-drying fabric glue for materials
Filler (for cushions or toys)
Braid or ribbon
Needle and thread
Tape measure

This box, having a simple circular interior, is easy to line and looks luxurious.

Cut out a circular piece of material approximately 3 cm (1¼ in) larger in diameter than the diameter of the interior of the box. (This is just a guideline and applies to a box of about 11 cm (4½ in) internal diameter and 4 cm (1½ in) deep.) Then about ½ cm (¼ in) down from the edge of the material, sew a running stitch right round the material, and pull the cotton in order to gather the material. Now place a small amount of filler in the box and drop the lining on top and ease the gathering evenly all round the wall of the box. With the tacky glue applied just under the gathered part of the material, stick the lining to the inside wall of the box about ½ cm (¼ in) down from the top edge of the box.

Finally, glue some decorative braid or ribbon all round the inside of the box on top of the rough, cut edge of the material in order to hide it. Voilà — a rich-looking lining.

6

Découpage Under Glass

This technique is known to have been practised centuries ago by the Chinese, who applied silk under glass. In more recent times it was practised by the French, who liked to copy the appearance of Sèvres china.

In due course it became the rage of the Victorians during whose era it was known as Potichomania. They loved to produce pieces that looked like the expensive porcelain that was being collected by the rich and the aristocracy. By placing prints behind glass and then painting the background, the object was cleverly given the glazed look of porcelain and china.

Découpage under glass plays magical tricks on the eyes. Many wonderful effects can be achieved with paper backgrounds or paint. The observer of a finished piece may be fooled into thinking the object really is porcelain because of its smooth, translucent appearance.

A background of rice paper creates a delicate transparent look, while a woody mulberry paper lends itself wonderfully to botanical or insect prints.

This form of découpage is particularly popular with those who suffer from arthritis or repetitive strain injury (RSI) because in this method there are no layers of varnish to sand.

DECOUPAGE ON A GLASS PLATE

The following instructions for découpage on a glass plate show how backgrounds of either paint or rice paper may be applied.

Please see page 36 for the list of basic materials you will require for every découpage project. In addition, for découpage under glass, you will need the following:

ADDITIONAL MATERIALS

Papers of your choice
Thin rice paper or mulberry paper (optional)
Clear glass object — a plate, a bowl, a paperweight, a sheet of glass which can be framed as a picture, or thick bevelled glass suitable for a tablemat
Chinagraph pencil or coloured Pentel
Household paint or artist's acrylic paint: your choice
Cellulose paper paste, eg wallpaper paste or a similar clear, slow drying glue. Alternatively a PVA glue mixed with a very little glycerine or a gel medium with good adhesive qualities (see *Brand Names* page 91)

Découpage under glass with a painted background. Created by a member of the National Guild of Découpeurs (USA).

Water-based varnish and oil-based
   varnish
Gesso (if painting the background)
Vinegar or methylated spirits
   (optional)
(See *Materials* on page 16 for more
   details about the above materials.)
Sealer (e.g. Jo Sonia's All Purpose
   Sealer)

PAPERS

It is important that they do not have a very shiny surface such as the plastic finish of many modern wrapping papers because often glue does not adhere evenly to it. Also the paper should have a flat, not grained, surface and be of good quality, not too thick but at the same time does not need to be as thin as is necessary when being used under varnish as the paper is not being 'sunk'. Avoid thin paper with print on the back.

TECHNIQUE

Make sure the surface on to which you are going to apply your prints is squeaky clean. A good way to clean glass is with a mixture of 2 parts water to 1 part vinegar, or with detergent and water (rinse thoroughly), or even methylated spirits, although this can leave a bloom on the glass which must be polished off. Ammonia and water can be used as another alternative.

Choose prints and then seal the *back* of the print — *never seal the front of the print for découpage under glass*. If using prints from magazines or books, check that there is no likelihood of newsprint bleeding through (for more information see page 39).

Cut out and prepare the prints in the usual way (see Choosing Your Prints, page 39, Cutting, page 24, and Cutting Out, page 39).

DESIGNING YOUR COMPOSITION AND APPLYING THE CUT-OUTS

Work on a piece of waxed paper so that when you come to apply glue to your prints they will not stick to the surface on which you are working.

Place your cut-outs under the glass and move them around until you are happy with the composition. Trace their position on to the top of the glass with your chinagraph pencil. Alternatively you may wish to cut out a paper template of the plate and move the prints around on the template before deciding on your design. Having made your decision, place the prints in position under the plate and

Once your glass object is squeaky clean and your prints have been selected, sealed *on the back*, and cut, arrange them under the glass until you are satisfied with the design. *Trace the position on top of the glass with a chinagraph pencil.*

then trace these positions on top of the plate with a chinagraph pencil.

Put the cut-outs to one side.

Apply a generous amount of cellulose paste (or other suitable medium) on to the *face* of a cut-out and stick it in position under the glass plate. Alternatively, you may leave the print face up on the waxed paper and then lift the paper up with the print on it, and place it against the glass. Press it gently to the glass, then carefully take the paper away. Some people like to put the pasted print on a damp kitchen sponge and lift the print up and apply it to the glass that way.

Next, with a damp, but not wet, sponge pat the print gently against the glass. Do this looking at the print from the front of your plate because it is important to detect the presence of any little air bubbles. These appear as shiny spots between the glass and the face of the print. If you see them, gently tease them out to the edge of the paper with the back of your fingernail, and release them. Be very careful not to press out the paste as you do this or you will end up with unsightly patches on the face of the print when the paste has dried.

Turn the plate over and make sure no pieces of paper have torn and, most importantly, that there are no pleats in the paper. This happens easily with delicate and thin portions, like twigs and stems.

You will be delighted to know that you can overlap prints to get a special effect if you wish because there are no layers of varnish to think about! However, if you are going to overlap prints, remember that the print that is to appear in front on the face of the glass must go on first.

Continue the gluing process until you have completed your design. Then gently wipe off all excess paste from the glass surface and put the plate aside to dry for 24 hours.

When dry, take a toothpick and check that all edges are well stuck down, especially those areas that are overlapping. Also, by holding the plate to eye level, check to see if any tiny pieces are raised. If some pieces have not stuck down properly you can apply a little fast-drying PVA glue to a small area with your toothpick and leave to dry. Never use a roller on glass!

Make sure you remove all surplus glue and the glass surface is really clean before moving to the next stage.

APPLYING A PAPER BACKGROUND

If you decide to use a paper background, very attractive effects can be achieved, especially if the choice of paper is co-ordinated with the prints.

Fruit designs, for example, look particularly effective with a mulberry paper, while romantic or ethereal themes such as fairies or cherubs look most attractive with thin patterned rice papers that incorporate fine designs such as flowers or cobwebs. Many rice paper table napkins are suitable and rice paper comes in many colours. Remember, whatever paper

When you have glued the prints to the *back* of the plate, decide whether you want a rice paper or painted background.

For a rice paper background, tear your chosen paper into small pieces and apply with paste or glue to the back of the glass, covering the previously applied prints. Overlap the edges of the paper slightly and continue until the surface is covered. Allow to dry, trim and seal with 3 coats of varnish.

you choose, it is best to use a thin paper.

Tear the rice or mulberry paper into fairly small pieces. Then apply a generous amount of paste to the back of the glass, and behind the prints. Stick down the patches of paper, overlapping the edges very slightly, until the entire surface is covered. Pat into place with your sponge and remove any air bubbles as before (see page 22).

When dry — 24 to 48 hours — trim any excess paper protruding over the edge of the glass and make sure the perimeter edge is well stuck down.

Next, seal the back of the plate with a varnish, making sure it goes over the paper on the edge of the plate; this will help to stop water seepage.

If the object is to be used for purely decorative purposes, simply apply 3 coats of a water-based varnish. But if you wish to use your plate, add an additional coat of an oil-based varnish. Be sure to use one that does not yellow as this will detract from the appearance of the rice paper, especially if it is white.

At all times wash the plate carefully. Do not put it in a dishwasher or very hot water.

A second technique is to apply *thin* rice paper to the back of the plate first, and *then* apply the prints behind it.

If you use this method, the prints must be in strong colours so as to show through the rice paper clearly. You can then glue another layer of rice paper behind the print — try using a different colour — but make sure that the overlapping edges are very fine.

Alternatively, just paint behind the

rice paper. This use of rice paper creates a soft dreamy appearance.

APPLYING A PAINTED BACKGROUND

A painted background will make your finished glass object look like a piece of china. An oil-based paint (either household or artist's paint) has the best adhesive quality, but it takes longer to dry. Household water-based paint can be used, as can artist's acrylic paint, but there is always a danger that the latter might eventually crack.

Before painting the background, apply a *thin* coat of sealer or water-based varnish over the whole back surface of the plate.

Some sealers adhere better to glass than others so it is preferable to buy

Finished découpage under glass showing a rice-paper background (left) and a painted finish.

Before applying a painted background, coat the back of the glass and prints with sealer or water-based varnish and allow to dry well. *Apply at least 3 coats of paint and leave to dry thoroughly before finishing with several coats of gesso, paint, and then varnish.*

one that is recommended for use on glass. However, as long as you allow the sealer or varnish to dry thoroughly, it should work.

Pay careful attention to any paper that overlaps another piece, making sure you cover it well — this prevents paint seeping under the glass and on to the face of your print, which can lead to tears!

Leave the sealer to dry for 4 days.

Now apply at least 3 coats of paint behind the prints, allowing plenty of drying time between each coat. (See *Tips* on drying — page 25.) Sometimes the paint may lift as you apply it. Just stop, let it dry for 4 days, apply another coat of sealer and let that dry well. Then carry on painting.

The painted back of the plate will not look very attractive as the prints will stand out in relief. If the object is going to be used and the underside or outside will be on view — such as

More examples of découpage under glass. From left: two rice paper finishes; a smoked and painted background; a mulberry paper background; and (front) plastic finger plates for a door and a small glass box.

with a plate or bowl — apply a number of layers of gesso (see page 16) until the prints are 'sunk'. It is essential that you put the gesso on thinly so that it can dry out well because it is going on to a non-porous surface. Finally apply a couple of coats of paint in the colour of your choice.

If you have decorated a bowl so that you see the inside, you may wish to add a few more prints to the outside. Seal the painted outside surface, attach the cut-outs and finish with varnish in the usual way.

If, however, you are not applying further prints, just cover your surface with 3 layers of varnish.

Alternatively, acrylic paint may be added to gesso and used as a background paint straight on to the glass behind the prints. Remember, though, the colours when mixed with gesso will naturally be pale. A dreamy, subtle look can be achieved by not stirring the paint very thoroughly into the gesso so that the colour appears in streaks throughout.

OTHER PAINTED EFFECTS

Many pleasing effects can be achieved with background paints. After you have gained confidence in applying a plain painted background, it is fun to experiment with other finishes. Practise first on samples of glass.

Try lightly sponging on one colour and then sponging on one or two more before painting a final background colour.

Dip the tip of a soft paint brush into the paint and then, with a swirling movement, streak it over the glass surface before applying the background colour.

Bronze powders sprinkled into the wet sealer before applying coats of paint can be very effective, as is the use of metallic paints in conjunction with each other.

Metallic waxes are also wonderful to use on glass. They come in varying shades and can be mixed to superb effect. Dip a polybrush in turpentine and rub in the wax, then apply to the glass. Leave to dry 24 hours.

Finally, when any of these painting methods are complete, apply coats of varnish as described above.

These techniques can be used on any glass and acrylic objects (but don't use turps on acrylic). A curved surface such as a bowl can be awkward to glue prints on because it is difficult to prevent wrinkles. To avoid this keep your prints small, or cut tiny nicks in unobtrusive places to facilitate a flat cut-out.

SMOKED GLASS

An interesting effect can be achieved with smoked glass. Hold a knife in the flame of a candle until black smoke appears, then wave the piece of glass through it until you have achieved a smoky appearance to your taste.

Holding a can of spray sealer or fixative well away from the glass, give a fine spray of sealer over the smoke on the plate to bond and settle it. This needs to be done about 3 times with care. If you spray too closely or heavily the smoke will disperse or run.

When dry apply background paint or rice paper.

7

Lining a Box

There are many schools of thought on how to line a box, and hard and fast rules cannot be made here about measurements since there are many factors involved. You must use your own judgement. Some people favour other slightly different techniques in the cutting and gluing of the material; however, all are in their own way satisfactory.

Two considerations to take into account are:

a. the thickness of the material you plan to use

b. the type of lid fitting — it may, if hinged, sit flat on the base of the box, or, alternatively, it may have a lip so that it fits into the box.

The following is an easy way to line a box with a hinge, where the lid sits flush on the base.

See also a different technique for lining a round box on page 56.

MATERIALS

A lined box is even more attractive than a painted interior. When you have put a lot of time and trouble into decorating the outside of a box, it deserves a beautiful lining. So choose a material or paper that complements the colour and pattern of the outside decoration. Velvet, velveteen, gros grain, satin, taffeta or heavy silks are all suitable fabrics, while marbled or simple decorative papers can also be used. Finish the lining off with a border of braid or ribbon. However, while the lining is important, always remember that it is secondary to the external decoration of the box.

Material for lining: velvet is ideal as it looks rich, fits snugly and hides any little slip-ups. Do not use a thin silk — it marks very easily

Tacky glue — or a thick, fast drying, non-staining fabric glue that dries clean such as Tarzan's 450

Thin firm cardboard

Padding as used for quilting, or stuffing as used for cushions

A reel of cotton

Tape measure/ruler

Large scissors

TECHNIQUE

LINING A SQUARE OR RECTANGULAR BOX

Measure the four internal lengths of the box, and then deduct 1 mm ($\frac{1}{16}$ in)

from two opposite sides, A1 and A2. Then measure the depth, deducting approximately 2 mm from the top.

Cut out four pieces of cardboard to these measurements. Put two pieces of cardboard (A1 and A2) into the box on opposite sides and make sure they fit, leaving about 1 mm at either end for the material to be folded round the ends (A1 and A2). Slip in the two remaining pieces of cardboard opposite each other, trimming their length so that they go in easily, without a gap, although leaving room again for fabric to be passed around (B and B1).

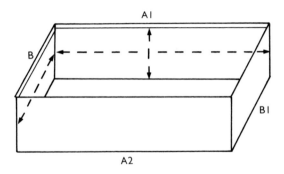

Cut cardboard measured to the 4 internal lengths of the box (less 1 mm/1/16 in from each of A1 and A2) and the depth (less 2 mm/1/8 in).

Remove the cardboard and place each section on the material. Cut out four separate pieces of material with a border of approx 15 mm (5/8 in) on the top and two sides, but cut the bottom flush with the cardboard.

Put a line of tacky glue along the bottom edge of the cardboard and stick the material firmly to the cardboard.

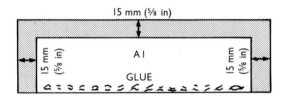

Glue each of the 4 pieces of cardboard to separate pieces of material, leaving a border of 15 mm (5/8 in) on each side, except the bottom which should be cut flush with the coardboard.

Next, mitre (cut off) both corners of the material, leaving a tiny fraction of material beyond the corners of the cardboard. Put a blob of tacky glue on the tip of the corners of the cardboard.

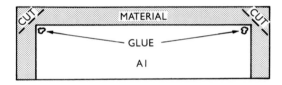

Cut off the corners of the material, leaving a small allowance between the corners of the cardboard.

Put tacky glue along the material border and then fold it over the cardboard and press down firmly. Ease in the fabric at the corners to make them clean and sharp.

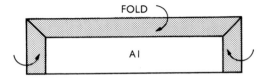

Apply glue to the corners of the cardboard and along the borders of the material, then fold the material over and press firmly to make sharp corners.

Put tacky glue on the inside walls of the box. Then put the completed linings into the box with the cardboard side against the wall. Press firmly to stick the linings in place.

Now take the inside base measurement of the box and cut out a piece of cardboard to that size. Drape a piece of cotton thread across the inside of the box, like a sling with the ends hanging over the sides of the box, and then drop the cardboard base into the box, over the cotton, to test for fitting. Remember you have to allow space all round for material. You can pull the base out by pulling up the cotton.

Cut a piece of padding to the size of the cardboard. Put a blob of glue at each corner of the cardboard and stick the padding to the cardboard, pressing down on the glued corners. Trim it in a bit at an angle from the edges.

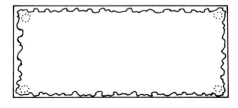

With a blob of glue at each corner, attach a piece of padding cut to the correct size to the cardboard.

Turn the cardboard over and place it, padding side down, on top of the wrong side of the fabric.

Cut out the material as before, leaving a 15 mm (⅝ in) border all around, and mitre the corners. Apply glue to the borders of the fabric and

fold over, pressing down firmly. Now put a little glue on the base of the box and drop the covered base in, right side of material face up. Press down firmly. There should be no gaps in the corners. If there are, glue braid over spaces to hide them, and do this over each corner.

Now you can line the lid of the box in the same way. Always measure the lid separately. If the sides of the lid are too small to line, just line the base of the lid, and glue braid or ribbon around the inside edges of the lid. Braid can also be an attractive finishing touch as a border around the top edge of the lining in the base of the box — it gives an even more luxurious appearance.

LINING A ROUND BOX

This is an alternative method to the one described in the chapter on *Basic Découpage Under Varnish* on page 45.

Measure the circumference and the depth of the box as in the instructions above. Cut out a long strip of thin cardboard to these measurements. It should fit with the two ends just butting together. Do not overlap them.

Place the cardboard down on the lining material and cut out, leaving a 15 mm (⅝ in) border on the top and sides.

Apply the glue along the bottom edge between the cardboard and fabric as before. Mitre the corners of the material, glue and fold over. Try to avoid wrinkles — leave under heavy books for a while.

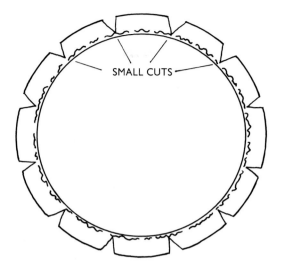

To make sure the fabric fits well over a round cardboard base, cut small nicks around the edges to provide 'give'.

Join the butting edges at the back with a bit of sticky paper. Make sure the unlined side of the cardboard faces out. Then place in the box, gluing the lining to the sides of the box. If the two butting edges do not meet neatly on the right side of the lining, cover with a decorative braid or ribbon.

Next, measure and cut out the round base in cardboard, allowing room for material, and test for size by dropping it into the box on a cotton sling (see page 55). Place the cardboard on the material, and cut out allowing a 15 mm (⅝ in) border.

Cut and glue the padding as previously described, then turn over and place on to the wrong side of the cut-out fabric.

Because the cardboard is circular, it is important to cut a series of nicks in the material all the way around so that the fabric lies flat when folded.

Apply the glue to the fabric border, fold the material over and press down.

Drop the completed lining into the box having applied a little glue to the base of the box beforehand.

If there is a gap between the base and side linings, cover with ribbon or braid.

8

Cloisonné and Illumination

The techniques of cloisonné and illumination are, after a little practice, quite simple to master and give a wonderful additional richness and excitement to your prints, and a fascinating extra dimension to découpage.

CLOISONNÉ

This form of découpage takes its name from the ancient technique also known as cloisonné from the French word 'cloison', which means 'a cell'. It was a method of multi-colour enamelling on pottery or metal in which intricate patterns were separated and outlined by thin metal threads, bands or fillets.

Cloisonné was superbly executed in the Byzantine era of the sixth century, and portrayed Christian themes of Christ, the cross and the saints. Concurrently it was found in Japan and later in China in the thirteenth century. The Japanese and Chinese depicted flowers and ornamental designs.

In sixteenth century Europe, Limoges was the centre for this form of enamelling, but then in the nineteenth century this technique seemed to fade in popularity. Today, however,

it has had a revival and fine contemporary examples are to be found again in Japan and China.

Please see page 36 for the list of basic materials you will require for every découpage project. In addition, for cloisonné, you will need the following:

ADDITIONAL MATERIALS

Thin bright gold paper or gold foil as used in chocolate wrappers. Preferably not those with a plastic finish. (This technique is generally followed by a diet!)

TECHNIQUE

Cloisonné in découpage works very well in conjunction with hand colouring (see page 64). Many of the scrolls and simple flower borders found in the Dover range of publications are very suitable for colouring.

If hand colouring, make coloured areas fairly solid, without too much gradation of tone. You should be trying to copy enamelling on real cloisonné objects, which often do not have much tonal change.

If you choose pre-coloured paper or

prints, Italian scroll designs or florals with fairly flat colouring and simple outlines, are preferable. Chinese and Japanese designs lend themselves to this technique as well. Human figures, animals and buildings, however, are not so suitable.

Seal the face of your prints and the coloured side of your gold paper.

Cut out the design and paint the edges, then glue down the cut-outs on to the gold paper. Now very cautiously and with a steady hand, cut around the design leaving a narrow border of gold, not more than 1 mm ($^1/_{16}$ in) wide. As you become more skilled you should aim to cut the gold strip about $^3/_4$ mm ($^1/_{20}$ in) wide (see photograph).

Paint the gold edges, then glue the print to the surface and *remove any excess glue with a sponge*. Sink the print in varnish as for Basic Découpage (see page 42), but remember to apply more coats than usual because there are two layers (the print and the foil) to sink.

To achieve the rich effect cloisonné can give, select your prints and some gold foil paper. Seal them all, then cut out and paint the edges of the prints. Glue them on to the gold foil. *Very carefully cut around the print, leaving a fine band of gold no more than 1 mm ($^1/_{16}$ in) wide. Always come up from underneath the print when cutting small internal areas.*

The result is that the whole outline of the cut-out will have a very fine gold border which represents the metal thread employed in real cloisonné. Remember to be subtle — too thick a gold border looks heavy and clumsy.

When complete, paint the edge of the gold paper, glue down (page 41) and varnish (page 42) in the usual way, but remember you will have to apply more coats of varnish than normal as you have two layers of paper to sink!

Examples of cloisonné.

ILLUMINATION

'First you see it, then you don't' — that is the essence of skilful and tasteful illumination. The effect must be subtle and delicate and never garish.

Think of the wondrous, sparkling colours of illuminated manuscripts — the glittering gold, the dazzling blues, yellows, reds and greens — and how they dance off the parchment or paper, which has been so expertly enhanced by the painter's brush.

In découpage it is a technique in which small slivers are cut out of your chosen print and are replaced with pieces of coloured foil that catch the light to illuminate, decorate and highlight the design of your print.

Illumination adds a rich dimension to découpage but must be employed in a restrained manner. Prints of flowers, butterflies, birds and clothing lend themselves beautifully to this form of decoration.

When illuminating a picture remem-

Hand-coloured prints with illumination and applied to a fabric background. Created by Joy Allbright.

ber not to overdo the colours used. It is often preferable to use only one or two colours although you could use a variety in the shades. Only in richly coloured designs should you get carried away and use many colours. Be careful not to over-decorate with colour — it can easily look cheap.

Please see page 36 for the list of basic materials you will require for every découpage project. In addition you will need the following:

ADDITIONAL MATERIALS

Thin coloured foil papers as used to wrap chocolates — gold, red, blue —

as many colours as possible. Preferably not those with a plastic finish.

TECHNIQUES

Before you start, be sure to seal the coloured side of your foil as well as sealing and cutting out your prints.

Now, consider your print. Some areas in an illustration or design cry out for illumination — a bird's eye; the streaks on its wing; the centre of a flower near the stamens; the shadow under a petal; the 'eyes' of a butterfly's wings; or the folds of the fabric of a dress.

For illumination, prepare the surface to be decorated, select and seal your prints as usual. As well, select variously coloured pieces of foil and seal them. Consider the print and select the areas to be highlighted by the illumination. *With a pin or scalpel, carefully make fine holes or cut slivers from the print.* Work from the front and remember it is better to cut too little than too much!

Paint the edges of the print, then decide which colours of foil you want to appear where on the print. *With a fine paint brush apply some glue around the holes in the print and attach the foil.* Press down with a damp sponge. Turn the print over to the right side and clean any excess glue from the surface of the foil. When all the holes have been illuminated and the glue is dry, attach the prints to the surface to be decorated and sink the print under varnish as in Basic Découpage (see page 42).

In the photograph, see how in the three-panelled gilded screen the gown comes alive when portions of the pattern are replaced by a glint of illumination. The already colourful garments light up with the added dazzling dimension of glittering foil.

Remember always that less is more, both in the amount of illumination and the size of the pieces you cut from the print.

Until you become adept at this technique, make an ordinary photocopy (or better still, a colour copy) of your print and experiment with where you want the illumination to be, and then practise the subtle cutting.

With a pin or a scalpel, and working from the front of the print, prick or cut out a fine sliver from the print. If you use a pin to make a tiny hole, cut off the 'collar' of paper that has been pushed through to the back of the print. Place a piece of coloured foil under the slit or hole and see how much glint from the foil appears.

If you have made the cuts too large, the effect will be clumsy and too obvious; if you have been too cautious, you will hardly catch a glimmer of foil at all — so experiment. It is better to cut too small and carefully enlarge the area than to slice too large a piece

The beautiful triptych screen showing fine illumination on Klimt prints.

which you cannot repair.

As well, play around with the pieces of foil to discover which colour works best in particular areas.

Once you have experimented on the copy, you can move on to the real thing. Ascertain where you want the colours to appear then cut out the slivers of print.

Paint the edges of the print where you have made the cuts. This is important because the white paper edge will show up very obviously against the bright foil.

Next, cut a patch of the foil you have decided to use. With a very fine paintbrush or a toothpick, put a tiny amount of glue around the hole or sliver (on the underside, of course!). Carefully place the patch down, patting firmly with your damp sponge.

Immediately turn your cut-out over to see if any glue has oozed out on to the coloured foil and, if so, wipe it off gently with the sponge or a cotton tip. Sometimes it can be scraped off with a toothpick. Do not let any glue dry on the coloured foil as it will deaden the colour and reduce the sparkle.

When everything is dry, glue your prints to the surface (see page 41) to be découpaged as usual and sink the print in with coats of varnish (see page 42).

9

Hand Colouring

As we have seen, traditional découpage was originally created using artists' hand-coloured drawings and engravings which were then cut out to decorate a multitude of different kinds of surfaces. In the early days of découpage, paints were used for hand colouring; it is only in recent times that oil pencils have been utilised. They are easier to use to greater effect and give more control than paints. Pencils are also more readily available to budding découpeurs.

Hand colouring as practised in the eighteenth century is the purest and most classical form of découpage. It widens the horizons of our creativity and is at the same time most absorbing and rewarding. It also gives greater flexibility to design as colours can be chosen to suit our own schemes and backgrounds as well as the nature of the prints being used.

It should be noted that hand-coloured prints and pre-coloured prints should not be used in conjunction with one another as they are generally of such different texture, appearance and character.

To be able to hand colour opens new doors. Dover Books have many publications produced especially for découpeurs to hand colour, but you can also colour black and white illustrations from other books, old prints, or photocopies of photographs and even touch up pre-coloured illustrations.

Hand colouring gives greater flexibility to your basic prints because by choosing the colours to use, the prints can be made to suit their surroundings. Start looking more carefully at paintings and study the selection of colours and nuances of light and shade. Study different styles and periods of art and become more colour conscious.

You should also have some basic knowledge of colour. (See the colour wheel opposite.)

Primary colours: red, yellow, blue
Secondary colours: a mixture of two primary colours
red + yellow = orange
yellow + blue = green
blue + red = violet
Intermediate or tertiary colours: a primary colour mixed with a secondary colour, e.g. yellow and orange, blue and green, red and violet.
Complementary colours: the two colours facing each other on the colour wheel, e.g. red and green. Two complementary colours mixed in equal parts will give a grey or neutral colour.
Warm colours: to the right of the red/

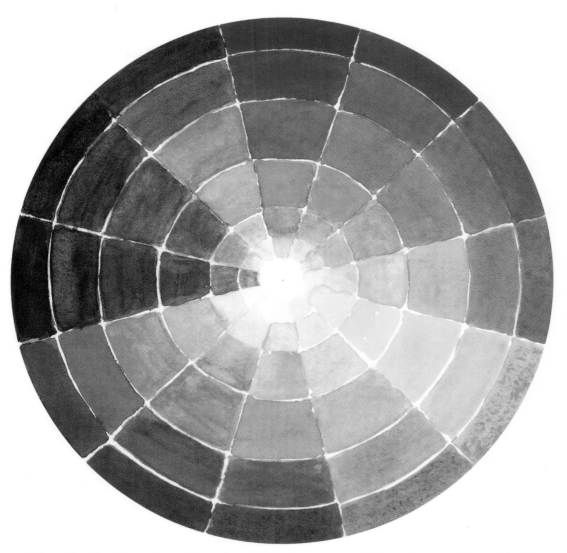

Colour wheel by Norma Carter. Reproduced by kind permission of Norma Carter and Anne Wheeler.

green axis are the warm colours (those with yellow and orange in them)

Cool colours: to the left of the red/ green axis are the cool colours (those with violet and blue in them)

All cool colours are harmonious and all warm colours are harmonious. In general warm and cool colours should not be juxtaposed since they do not sit harmoniously together. However, if you wish to introduce a warm colour into a group of cool colours, add a little of the complementary cool colour to the warm colour first to create a compatible contrast.

Tint (lighter value): a colour mixed with white (highlights)

Eighteenth-century figures surrounded by a floral *cartouche* on a tabletop. Created by a member of the National Guild of Découpeurs (USA).

Shade (darker value): a colour mixed with black (lowlights)

Both Hiram Manning and Patricia Nimmocks, two revered twentieth-century découpeurs, have written in detail about traditional palettes used in découpage. These are described in this chapter.

Shades of apricot and blue have been given the name of *Pompadour Palette*. These were the favourite colours of Madame de Pompadour and can be seen in many famous paintings of her.

François Boucher gave his name to the *Boucher Palette* of pale pinks, flesh colours and terracotta mixed with soft blues and greens.

The *Provincial Garden Palette* is reminiscent of the flowers of the French countryside and contains soft pinks, lilac, pale blues and greens.

The *Empire Palette* derives its name from Empress Josephine Bonaparte when the predominant and favourite furnishing colours of the time were ivory and gold, with warm wood colours and apple greens and blues.

Chinoiserie (fantasy Chinese) colours of the eighteenth century form a palette of bold peacock colours, strong blues and greens, ultramarine, violets, scarlet and yellows.

The *Eighteenth Century Palette* includes a wide range of colours, but the colours are carefully selected to harmonise and complement each other.

The *Toile de Jouey Palette* originated from French fabrics. With a traditional cream or white background, this is a monochromatic palette based on about three shades of whatever colour is being used, plus white. The usual combinations are red and white, blue

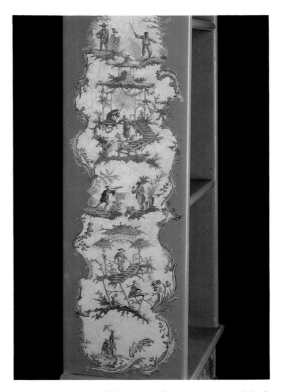

Hand-coloured Pillement figures on a gilded background on a display shelf. Created by Philippa Barbour.

Restored gilded eighteenth-century screen with glass panels and twentieth-century hand-coloured floral prints. Created by Joy Allbright.

and white, green and white, and deep indigo and white. Toiles are pictorial and generally tell a story, often historic, such as the fall of the Bastille, or the American Revolution.

The *Grisaille Palette* employs varying shades of grey (or a little blue), plus black, and blended with white. This palette is commonly used for architectural and sculptural illustrations.

Another such is the *Sanguine* (blood colours) *Palette* consisting of dark browns, terracotta, strong reds, some black, again blended with white to soften the colours so that they flow smoothly into each other.

Some of the most beautiful effects are best achieved by the subtle use of only a few colours, especially when using architectural drawings, scrolls and friezes of the Renaissance and Italianate style.

The beginner would be wise to start with a monochromatic or limited palette, say just three tints of one colour or three colours. Use a light pencil for the lightest area, a dark pencil for the dark areas and a medium and pure colour for in-between.

Experiment with different palettes, but be disciplined about keeping a note to one side of your print indicating which colours you have used. Do not be fooled into thinking you will remember because you won't, and it is frustrating when at a later date you wish to repeat those colours and then you can't recognise them!

It is a common mistake with beginners to use too many colours and the whole thing ends up looking a big colourful muddle with no theme or style. As a general rule it is better to use fewer colours rather than more. Be careful not to gild the lily. Decide before you start what colours you are going to use, select them and put any others out of temptation's way. Use your selected few. If you really feel an additional colour is needed, add it later.

HINTS FOR HAND COLOURING

- *The Golden Rule:* always keep your pencils well sharpened to a fine point. A finishing touch to a sharpened pencil can be to rub it against a fine sandpaper.
- Always work on a slightly soft

surface such as a pile of about four magazines — this will be firm but with some slight give.

- As a general rule, do not colour a nose, especially not one in profile!
- Until you are experienced, look at a picture and decide where in the picture the strongest light is coming from (i.e. how the areas of light and shade fall) and draw an arrow on the side of your paper to remind you.
- When colouring, constantly take into consideration the shape, angle of light and the outline. If you are colouring an engraving, follow the engraving lines to help you with shape and as a guide as you colour. You will, for example, use your darkest pencil where the engraving lines are heaviest. It is a good idea to go over any faint outlines of a drawing with a pencil first before you start colouring.
- To achieve perspective, remember that the objects or figures nearest to you are darker than those in the distance, which are lighter, so colour accordingly.
- Colours to be covered by varnish (especially under an oil-based varnish) need to be stronger than colours being placed under glass.
- Be sure to work in good light, and as far as possible do not colour when you are tired. If you have coloured when you are weary, or in bad light, you are sure to be disappointed with the results in the morning! Tired eyes can cause rough colouring and make you see the colour differently because they lose that sharpness for detail.

TRADITIONAL COLOURING

MATERIALS

Oil coloured pencils *not* watercolour (aquarelle)
A soft artist's rubber
A good pencil sharpener
A fine sandpaper (optional)

Having decided on your palette, begin to colour in the drawing being guided by the engraving lines, if present. The strokes of the pencil should go in the same direction as the lines.

The area where the engraving is heavy represents shade and here the colour should be dense or you should use dark tones. Where there is little or no engraving will be the area with the most light on the surface, and here you should use your palest colour or maybe just white. Where there are no engraving lines to guide you, then you must decide yourself where light and shade are falling and colour accordingly. Use white to add dimension to your colouring and to indicate where the light is striking most strongly on the object. Alternatively a pale yellow or beige can be used.

Do not be tempted to press hard with your pencil. A number of light, thin strokes is better than fewer, heavier thick strokes. It is very easy, if you are heavy-handed, to end up with a muddy mess! However, if you do, you can generally remove some of the colour with a good eraser.

Practise first. The movement of the pencil on the paper should be a light flick away from you, so that the first part of the stroke is heavy and then tapers off to the thinnest of lines as the pencil rises off the paper. Do a number of close strokes next to each other in this way so that they merge to create a solid area of colour rather than showing individual lines. Keep your touch *light*. If your pencil strokes are showing you are probably pressing too hard and holding your pencil too tightly — relax!

Hand colouring with oil-based pencils works particularly well on etchings and other black-and-white prints. Carefully choose a palette that suits the style of the print and also consider the background colour of the surface you will be decorating. *Use fewer colours to achieve a subtle effect (as shown in the blue leaves) and work with light flicking strokes. Do not press too hard or use a 'scrubbing' motion with the pencil. Use a white pencil to blend the colours, and accent with black or dark shades.*

Begin with the deepest colours in the darkest areas, then pull them out by blending one colour into the next

and so taper into the paler colours used in the lighter areas.

Use your white pencil constantly — you cannot live without it. The white pencil is essential to bring your colours to one another and to blend them to give a smooth finished look. Colour and blend with your white repeatedly, always using the same flicking movement of your pencil.

Do *not* go backwards and forwards with your pencil as a small child might; you will not achieve subtlety of colour and contrast that way.

When you are coming to the end of an area of colour, accent with black (using it with discretion), burnt carmine, raw umber or a darker shade of the original colour, but never use white over your dark accent lines.

With your dark accent pencils, you can also replace lines in the drawing — such as the veins in a leaf or the curls in a head of hair — that may have been lost under the colour. Also check to see if a little final touch of the white pencil might be needed to accentuate the lighter areas. Do not be afraid to leave the most highlighted areas totally white.

A stunning effect can be achieved with cross-hatching, particularly to create the impression of rich silks or satins of a woman's garments. Colour lightly with your pencil in one direction and then, with a contrasting colour, pencil lightly across the area at a different angle to give the appearance of shot silk.

Colour right to the outline of the drawing. Do not worry if you go over it, as you will be cutting the outline out and so a few slips won't matter.

ORIENTAL WOODBLOCK, ART DECO OR ART NOUVEAU PRINTS

MATERIALS

Tortillons or, if unavailable, paper blending pencils made of paper and used for pastels (torchons)
Mineral turpentine

You will notice that these are often painted with no effects of light and shade and are therefore flat and without dimension. For these illustrations colouring is much simpler and quicker (see photograph).

When choosing your colours, remember that while sombre colours are often used in Chinese and Japanese paintings, wonderful brighter colours were often found in their garments and carpets. Do not be frightened to use soft or bright colours.

Use a free hand with art nouveau and art deco illustrations, too, although as a general rule the colours for those styles did not normally tend to be very strong.

Now you can colour in a more basic way — back and forth, as you did as a child. Make a good solid colour with your pencils — right out to the edge of the drawing.

FINISHING

To finish, take your tortillon and dip it in the mineral turpentine and then rub the damp point over the coloured areas. The pencil marks become

For effects such as that of a Japanese wood block, you can *rub the damp tip of a tortillon dipped in mineral turpentine over the hand-coloured print*. This will help blend and smooth the colour. The blue flower shows the step-by-step stages of hand-colouring — adding colours progressively to a black-and-white drawing.

When you have finished, seal and cut out the print, paint the edges, glue to the surface and sink the print under varnish as for Basic Découpage (see page 42).

blended and smooth and the colour becomes richer. It is important not to touch the black lines if you have used a photocopy, as they have a tendency to smudge when in contact with turps. This warning also applies to some cheaper forms of printing.

After colouring and finishing with turps, seal and cut your prints out and proceed with whichever découpage technique you plan to use. Hand colouring works particularly well with *Basic Découpage Under Varnish* (see page 36), *Découpage Under Glass* (see page 47).

The finished jewellery box showing the use of hand-coloured prints.

10

Repoussé, Moulage and Tôle

REPOUSSÉ AND MOULAGE

You will no doubt have seen lacquered Chinese furniture and decorative objects with raised motifs — figures, birds, plants — which generally have also been gilded. It is partly from that Eastern craftsmanship that repoussé and moulage in découpage have been derived. This form of découpage breaks away from the traditional 'sunk' technique and is enormous fun to do.

Repoussé and moulage, two words which come from the French, to 'push back' and to 'mould' respectively, are more or less synonymous. The technique involves kneading or indenting areas of a print from behind to give a raised and sculptured effect on the face of the print. To hold these areas in relief, they are filled with a modelling material. Repoussé requires the edges of the print to be glued down to the surface on which it is placed, while moulage leaves the edges raised and supported by the mastic.

These relief decorations can be used on their own to decorate a flat surface or can be combined very effectively with découpage sunk under varnish.

When selecting your prints, look for cherubs, fully clothed figures, butterflies, birds, animals, fruit or flowers, because they all lend themselves so well to this technique. Choose prints that are not too complicated and make sure they are of a size suitable for the article you are planning to decorate.

For repoussé you may use just one moulded print to place on your painted background, but for moulage it is preferable to position a duplicate print, which will be the one you are moulding, on top of one already stuck down.

Please see page 36 for the list of basic materials you will require for every découpage project. In addition, for repoussé and moulage, you will need the following:

ADDITIONAL MATERIALS

Burnisher (modelling implement used by potters and leather workers. It has a sharp point at one end and a narrow spoon-shape at the other.)
Air-drying modelling material, or homemade mastic (see *Materials* page 17 for recipe)
Fast-drying glue (e.g. Aquadhere)
Slow-drying glue (e.g. Clag)
Tacky glue or a quick-drying clear glue suitable for fabric
Glaze and thinners (or you can use gloss varnish)
Waxed paper
Barrier cream

TECHNIQUE

Remember to put some barrier cream on your hands as they are going to become pretty messy with the modelling material.

If you are going to combine the repoussé with sunk prints, first design the whole project deciding which prints will be sunk and which will be raised. Then stick, varnish and sink the appropriate prints in the normal way (see *Basic Découpage* page 36.)

Repoussé figures of a toreador and bull on a smoked painted surface. Created by a member of the National Guild of Découpeurs (USA).

Having selected your prints to be sculptured, seal them with 2 coats of sealer as usual (see page 37) but do not use shellac. Liquitex Gloss Medium and Varnish is very suitable for this.

Cut out the prints and paint the edges.

Place the cut-outs against a window pane with the face of the print against the glass so the light shines through it and on the back lightly pencil in the areas you intend to raise.

You will find it necessary in some areas, such as petals of flowers or wings of birds, to cut nicks or incisions round the edges of the petal or into the wing of a bird to provide a little more 'give' for contouring.

Place your print face down on a plastic, slightly spongy place mat or similar soft surface, which in turn has been placed on a couple of soft magazines. With the spoon-shaped end of your burnisher, gently push from the centre and smooth out to the edges the areas you wish to raise, until you have the contour you desire.

In readiness, knead your moulding

Repoussé and moulage are used to create a sculptured effect. This works particularly well to emphasise, for example as here, the effect of folds of a dress.

Having prepared the surface to be decorated, selected and sealed your prints, cut the prints out. Mark on the back of the print the areas to be raised by holding the print against a window and sketching the areas in with a pencil on the back. *Then, place the print face down on a soft mat and, with the spoon-end of your burnisher, press and mould the areas that will stand in relief.*

material so that it is smooth and has no air pockets.

Turn your print over, and find the area that has been raised the most: this will contain the most filling. The areas next in height will have a little less moulding material, and so it will continue until some areas, i.e. the flattest areas, will contain the least moulding material.

If you are doing a human figure it is sometimes appropriate to stick the neck flat on to the surface while the head and shoulders contain mastic and are moulded.

When moulding the branches and leaves of a tree, create a feeling of perspective by adjusting the amount of mastic in various areas.

As well you should decide which edges of the print will remain raised as moulage and stick the mastic right to the edge of the print.

Now, turn the print face down on a piece of waxed paper. Brush a good coat of glue (1 part slow-drying to 2 parts fast-drying) on to the back of the print. Then place pieces of mastic moulded into appropriate shapes in proportion to the sizes of the raised area.

Apply more glue to the surface of the moulding material and paper, turn it over and put it on the surface to be decorated. Put a damp paper towel over the print and leave it for about 5 minutes to soften the paper and make it more pliable.

With the spoon-end of your burnisher, gently push and mould the print, helping it with your free fingers

Apply glue to the back of your print. Prepare your moulding material — or mastic — by kneading it. *Then mould small pieces to sit in the areas depressed by your burnisher. The mastic will hold the areas in relief when the print is turned face-up.*

Apply more glue to the mastic before turning the print over and sticking it on to the surface. The mastic will hold the areas in relief when the print is turned face-up. *With your burnisher and fingers, carefully mould from above the mastic which is under the print so that it forms the shapes you desire.*

as you go along. In the photograph you will see the raised areas and valleys form the folds of a dress.

Gently mould with your fingers and your burnisher until you are satisfied with the appearance. The sharp end of the burnisher can be used to define thin lines and push back areas more sharply. Press down the edges of your print firmly to the surface and remove any excess moulding material with the sharp end of your burnisher. Clean away superfluous moulding material with a damp sponge or cotton tip. You have now created a piece of repoussé.

MOULAGE

You will see in the photograph that the hem of the woman's dress flies free from the surface, likewise her lace collar and the other woman's bonnet. These are supported by the moulding material so that they appear more three-dimensional. This is moulage.

When you were applying the piece of mastic to the print, you will have decided which edges were to remain raised as moulage when placing the print in position. Instead of sticking all the edges of the print down as in repoussé, the mastic is positioned right to the edge of the print. Once the print is in place and properly moulded, fix the areas of moulage. Scrape the wall of exposed mastic so that it recedes a little under the edge of the print and does not therefore protrude obviously.

When this is dry, paint that moulding material in a colour to match the print above it.

Moulage is the technique of making the edges of your print remain raised rather than being stuck down on the surface. Mastic is used to support and raise the edge. It works well for raised petals. *The mastic must be painted to tone in with print as shown here.*

———————

In the photograph of the small pink flowers you will see they have been treated in the same way. Here we have stuck a duplicate of the flower under the raised one so that the raised print reflects the one already glued to the surface beneath it. This is not absolutely essential but it does give a neater and more defined outline.

Clean up excess material as previously.

FINISHING

When the moulding material has dried hard (after about 48 hours) and you have painted the exposed mastic in the areas of moulage, you are ready to varnish.

The finished writing box showing repoussé, moulage and tôle. The latter can be seen as a decoration on the little box and the small shoe. It is the technique of leaving the moulded edges raised and free while the centre of the print is held in place with a little fast-drying glue.

Apply at least 8 coats of varnish to the raised areas. Be careful to apply the varnish thinly to the moulded areas to stop it sitting thickly and building up in dips and hollows. Some of the thinner water-based varnishes are best used here.

You can achieve a lovely finish after varnishing using 0000 wire wool or a car-cutting compound; with so few coats of varnish over the print this is safer than sanding. However, repoussé and moulage lend themselves to a gloss finish, so it can be very effective to apply a gloss finish only to the moulded areas in contrast to leaving the surrounding flat areas to be treated with a satin finish. These areas should be sanded very gently and then polished as usual (see page 44).

TÔLE

Paper tôle is quite a large subject in itself. In the photograph (opposite) a shoe and small box illustrate a simple and effective form of this technique. In tôle, different parts of a print are manipulated to emulate real life. For example, as here, small flowers may be cut out, and the petals and leaves moulded to shape, some up, some curling under.

Do this with the spoon end of your burnisher; the sharp end can then be used to score fine lines, depicting the veins in leaves and petals.

With tweezers, pick up the flowers and leaves, for example, and, putting a little blob of Tacky Glue under them, place them where appropriate. They should dry in shape. When firmly positioned, paint the petals and leaves with a few coats of gloss varnish or, more appropriately, with découpage glaze, which is used in the decoration of eggs and for the creation of three-dimensional paper tôle pictures. This hardens the paper to a porcelain-like glossy finish.

11

Other Projects

There is no end to the surfaces that can be découpaged as long as they are flat — so keep your mind and eyes open for ideas. Here are just a few.

DECOUPAGE ON SILK

This technique does not, of course, involve any varnishing. However, you must first spray the silk with Scotchguard or a similar protective product.

Examples of découpage showing the broad variety of its effects. The silhouettes hanging on the wall have been produced using découpage, and so have the decorations on the mirror frame and on the silk lampshade and the base.

Most commonly découpage on silk is applied to lampshades or framed pictures, although it is also possible to découpage parasols, screens, dressing table sets, tablemats (hessian or cotton), boxes and wall hangings. It goes without saying that objects decorated in this manner can only be used for ornamental purposes and must be treated with care, unless protected by glass.

MATERIALS

Papers of your choice — but without any print on the back
Silk object

TECHNIQUE

The following technique is the most successful for silk or fabric.

Cut your prints in the normal manner *but do not seal them first*. Place them face down on waxed paper and paint the backs with a heavy coating of white PVA glue but be careful they do not stick to the paper. It is likely that the prints may curl, and if this happens you can paint half the back of the print with glue and when dry, paint the other half.

Hand-coloured prints on a silk fan. Created by a member of the National Guild of Découpeurs (USA).

Let the prints dry thoroughly and then start planning the arrangement. You can temporarily adhere the prints to the silk using a non-staining removable adhesive such as Blu-Tack, but only press them on lightly. When you are happy with your design put a small dab of glue under each print to hold it in place. Allow the glue to dry.

Now heat an iron to medium — not too hot — be careful! With a thin, damp cloth under the iron, press the print to the silk, lifting the cloth away quickly or it will stick to the print. Press the print down with your fingers and repeat the exercise if there are any loose pieces that do not adhere.

When you have finished check that everything is well stuck down. If not, apply some more glue under the print with a toothpick and when dry, re-iron. It is essential when executing découpage on silk that the prints are very firmly stuck down.

You can use this technique on other fabrics, except, of course, those with a raised pile such as velvet.

In the case of the lampshade shown in the photograph, a slightly different technique was used. The faces of the prints were sealed. Then a good coat of fabric glue was applied to the print making sure it was taken well out to the edge of the print. However, care was taken not to use so much that it would ooze out and show on the silk. The prints were then very firmly pressed into place.

DECOUPAGE ON PORCELAIN AND BISQUE

PORCELAIN

By doing découpage on porcelain you avoid having to worry about background painting. Choose a pleasing shape and an object that is in keeping with the prints you wish to use, or vice versa. This particularly applies to vases, urns, ginger jars and so forth. Don't, for example, put an elongated print on a round, fat vase.

TECHNIQUE

Make sure the surface is spotlessly clean (see page 48 on glass preparation). Then give the surface the lightest sand with fine sandpaper.

Apply a coat of sealer suitable for glass. Sealer adheres better than many varnishes on this kind of surface and gives a base on to which the varnish will cling. Allow to dry for 4 days.

Now apply the cut-outs in the usual manner using a PVA glue (see page 41).

Apply varnish (see page 42). An oil-based varnish normally adheres to porcelain more satisfactorily than a water-based one, but remember it will be more yellowing so consider how it will affect the colour of your prints.

After you have applied most of your coats of varnish, you can add gold braid or gold strips of Letraset as an additional decoration. You need only apply a few more coats of varnish over the braid. Try to avoid sanding it; if necessary gently rub with wire wool. Braid does not need to be sunk.

BISQUE

Bisque is unglazed white porcelain and is porous. When you are buying a piece make sure that the joins have been removed by the potter and that it has been cleaned. Check that there is no distortion and that lids, where they exist, are in good shape and fit well.

A collection of bisque vases and ginger jars painted and decorated with découpage under varnish. Created by Val Lade.

If you want the object to be water-proof, for example, ensure the inside is glazed. If not, then make it water-proof by applying 3 coats of an oil-based gloss varnish.

TECHNIQUE

Sand well with a 320 garnet paper and clean with your tack cloth.

If you plan to use oil paint to decorate the surface, you must seal it first, preferably with a sealer especially suitable for bisque. Some découpeurs say that if you use acrylic paints sealing is not necessary because they act as a sealer themselves. I would always be happier to play safe and seal the surface.

Alternatively, for a really beautiful finish an application of at least 6 coats of gesso is ideal. (See Gesso page 16). When applying gesso to bisque it is advisable to paint a thin layer of acrylic sealer between coats.

Paint the gesso and decorate with prints in the normal way.

If you wish to decorate a vase or jar with bands of different painted colours, measure from the top of the vase or jar to where you want the band of paint to go, then draw a faint pencil line around the object at the desired positions. Attach masking tape along the line, either above or below it, according to where you wish to add the painted band. This isolates the areas to be painted and protects those that will not be. Make sure the masking tape is well pressed down to prevent the paint leaking underneath it. Then paint the area above or below in the colours desired. When the paint is dry, gently pull the tape off.

DECOUPAGE ON A MIRROR

This is fun to do but the drawback is that it really only works successfully on very thin mirror glass such as that used in a powder compact or on the wing mirror of a car. This is not easy to come by. The necessity for such thin glass is that normal mirrors reflect the back of the print which is detracting and unsightly. A test is to put your finger on the glass and if there is any space in the reflection

Découpage on a mirror by a member of the National Guild of Découpeurs (USA).

between your finger and its reflection, then don't use it.

TECHNIQUE

When you have found some suitable glass, paint or pencil the back of your prints black — this is essential.

Clean your mirror very thoroughly with soap and water, or ammonia and water, using a lint-free cloth or tissue paper to wipe it dry.

Decide upon your composition, then mark the position of your print on the mirror with a small guiding line or two with a chinagraph pencil. Remove the marks with water as you place your prints down.

Apply glue to the back of each print. Do not spread the glue, just dot a small blob here and there, enough to keep it in place.

When you have finished, place a cleaned piece of thin picture frame glass, which you have had cut to the same size, over the mirror. This keeps the prints in place and protects them from dirt and wear and tear. The two pieces of glass should be placed in a frame that has a deep enough rabbet to hold the two of them. Ask your picture framer for advice.

DECOUPAGE ON SOAP

This is quick but fun and many serious découpeurs have looked disapproving at the very thought. However, it need not look kitsch or cheap. Like all découpage, as long as the prints chosen and the design used are tasteful, then there is a place for it. Découpaged soap is a useful little gift and can look very pretty in the bathroom!

Use a soap with a smooth surface (no imprint) and preferably coloured, as white becomes discoloured by the varnish and is not so attractive.

TECHNIQUE

Apply 2 coats of a PVA glue on to the top of the soap, bringing it halfway down at the sides. Then seal your prints with 2 more coats of PVA and glue them to the soap.

Apply about 4 coats of a water-based acrylic varnish on top of the prints and soap, bringing it halfway down on the sides. Allow at least 24 hours between coats to dry. Leave for about 3 days to dry out well, and then — hey presto into the bathroom with it! The print will stay and the soap will wear away underneath.

You can also use oil-based varnish but it does discolour the soap slightly.

DECOUPAGE ON SHELLS

Shells, with their sand-worn surfaces and their soft and subtle colours, are very pleasing surfaces to découpage. Their natural colours can be a wonderful background to prints.

Shells are easy to paint and metallic and transparent paints look wonderful on them. Both the outside and the inside of the shells can be decorated as can be seen in the photograph. The inward curve of a shell creates a natural frame into which to place an image.

Seal whichever surface of the shell you want to decorate with a water-based sealer. Glue down the prints and varnish and polish in the normal way.

Small shells with pierced holes at the top can be used to make jewellery such as pendants and earrings. Cut out a tiny decorative object like a butterfly, fish or bird and with a toothpick put a couple of minute blobs of silicone behind them so that they can stand out in three-dimensional relief, as an alternative to gluing them down.

GOLD LEAF TRANSPARENCY

This is a relatively modern technique and is simpler to do than it might appear. The richness of the gold makes a striking contrast against the black lines of the print and gives the découpage an air of opulence (see photograph).

The following instructions for laying gold leaf have been simplified and are not the techniques used for more professional gilding. Nevertheless, these instructions are adequate for our requirements, and are meant for découpeurs who have no knowledge of gilding and have not used Dutch metal before and who do not necessarily wish to buy the tools normally required for gilding.

MATERIALS

Black and white prints which *must* have strong black lines (this can

Découpage on shells and on a beautifully decorated egg.

generally be achieved by darkening a print on a photocopier). Until you become adept at applying gold metal leaf, choose small prints

Gold metal leaf (this is not pure gold leaf and is often just referred to as Dutch metal)

Gold size (adhesive for gold leaf) — quick drying

Mod Podge or Liquitex Gloss Medium and Varnish or a similar water-based varnish/sealer (available at most crafts shops)

Natural sponge

Poly brush (a sponge brush on a handle) or soft paint brush

Flat, soft sable paint brush for laying leaf

Large pair of scissors

The small box in front shows découpage using gold-leaf transparency. It is flanked by two objects exhibiting découpage covered with a crackle-finish medium and two doorknobs. Behind is an antique country writing slope.

TECHNIQUE

First make a transfer. Apply at least 6 coats of varnish to the face of the print, leaving plenty of time between coats so that they dry thoroughly. Apply the coats in alternate directions and be careful not to leave any ridges. Leave for 24 hours.

Place the print in tepid soapy water and leave to soak for at least two hours. Now place the print face down on a smooth, firm surface and gently rub the back of the print with your sponge or finger, carefully removing the backing layers of paper. Be very careful not to rub too vigorously. When you have removed much of the paper, hang the print up to dry with a peg, or if it curls, press a portion of it against a flat, vertical surface.

When the print has dried for about 3 hours, soak it again for about 30 minutes and then continue to rub the back very carefully until all the paper has gone — but don't remove the black lines! You should now have a translucent transfer that looks the same on both sides. Make sure there are absolutely no little rough bits of paper left as these will show when you apply the Dutch metal. Leave it to dry thoroughly as before, then apply a thin coat of water-based varnish and leave to dry flat for a further 24 hours.

Place the transfer face down on a piece of wax paper and with your poly brush apply a coat of gold size, brushing both ways so as to be sure to get complete coverage.

There are various brands of gold size; some are ready to use in 10 minutes, while others take some hours.

To test for exactly the right moment to apply the gold metal leaf, bend your finger and lightly touch the size with your knuckle. If there is a 'click' as you lift it off, the moment has arrived. Don't go away and forget about it — keep checking, for you can easily pass the point of no return!

Be sure you are not in a draught and there is no breeze to blow your leaf away — this can happen easily!

With a large pair of scissors, and keeping a piece of tissue paper (which comes with the metal leaf) on top, cut the leaf into squares — not too small. Judge the size of the squares by the size of the print being gilded.

The next stage takes practice. Since at first you will only be applying small pieces of leaf to your print, you should be able to pick up a corner of the leaf delicately with tweezers or even with your fingers, placing it gently on the size. Pat it down carefully with the soft sable brush (kept especially for the purpose) but don't actually brush it.

If you have any bare patches after the application of the leaf, rub the brush against your cheek and, with the static created, pick up any little spare broken pieces of metal leaf — known as 'skewings' — and place them on the damp sized patches.

When the back of the print has been completely covered with the leaf, leave it to dry for about 30 minutes. Then gently brush it smooth with your soft brush but *do not* brush across and against the leaf edges as you may tear them.

An alternative technique to lifting and laying single sheets of Dutch metal is to use transfer gold leaf which comes attached to tissue paper. This is much easier for the beginner to use. It is, however, a little more expensive.

Finally, apply a coat of sealer — preferably shellac.

You now have a gold transfer which you can cut out and use as a normal print.

12

A Whole New World

Well, hasn't it been fun? Are you still in one piece? You possibly had a few dramas but none of them were unsurmountable I feel sure — anyway you've learnt what not to do next time! I hope you are delighted with what you have achieved because you have discovered a whole new artform and you are just beginning — the world is your oyster!

Don't be harsh on yourself if you can see faults, after all it is probably your first attempt and you should be very proud of your creation. It has been a learning process but most of all you have discovered new artistic depths within yourself. I hope you are hooked! Where else could you find a creative pastime that offers you the challenges, the joy and satisfaction, the potential for boundless originality, the fun and the creative fulfillment, in short, so many new pastures? It *is* a 'whole new world' you have entered.

Découpage often has its lighter moments, too. I sometimes think a fly on the wall in our classes would be somewhat puzzled by the dialogue. I recall a very shy, quiet bachelor who barely uttered to his fellow students. He was creating a wonderful box of religious paintings. When I asked him if he had had a nice weekend, he answered very seriously, 'No, not really, it was very disappointing. I spent the whole time looking for a virgin, but I couldn't find one *anywhere*.'

On another occasion a woman in the class was designing a child's chair. She had cut-outs spread around the dining room when her son entered through an outside door. The wind blew her work in all directions. Everything was found except the precious dragon — the centrepiece of the project. After many hours she gave up the search frustrated and disappointed. However, two weeks later she rushed into the class joyously announcing, 'I've found my dragon! He was quite okay and was sitting on top of the curtain'.

There is no limit to the confusion some people get themselves into until they are accustomed to all the materials we use. I remember a student who got muddled between glue and varnish. She stuck down her prints with varnish (not such a problem) but then painted 20 layers of glue on her box and became distressed because whenever she wet-sanded her 'varnish' it became a gooey, horrible mess and the whole thing looked a sorry sight. Nevertheless we were able to repair and disguise the damage and both the box and its creator lived to see another découpage day.

So I just wish you many happy, absorbing, exciting and creative hours with découpage. Keep hording paper and keep searching for those interesting, beautiful and unusual objects to decorate — I know you'll have fun.

Let me finish with a car sticker dreamt up by one of my fellow Guild members in America — 'Découpeurs don't die, they just cut out'.

Glossary

ACRYLIC
A fast-drying water-based paint or varnish

ART NOUVEAU
A style of design, art and architecture of the late nineteenth century

BAROQUE
A theatrical, grotesque and whimsical form of architecture and ornamentation of the seventeenth and eighteenth century

BIEDERMEIER
A heavy Germanic decorative style of interior design and decoration

BRAYER
A roller (preferably rubber) which is used to flatten a print and remove excess glue after adhering a print

BYZANTINE
An art form and architectural style that flourished in Byzantium (Constantinople) during the fifth and sixth centuries

CARNAUBA
A high-grade wax made from a palm leaf and used for final polishing

CARTOUCHE
An architectural decoration of the Renaissance period consisting of scrolls enclosing a space or motif

CHINAGRAPH PENCIL
A soluble pencil used for tracing purposes on porcelain or glass

COMPLEMENTARY COLOURS
Any two colours directly opposite each other on the colour wheel

CRACKLE
A medium used in conjunction with two coats of paint which causes the top coat to crack or craze

DECOUPAGE
The art of decorating surfaces with cut-out paper, traditionally under many layers of varnish

DECOUPEUR
A person who practises découpage

DISTRESSING
A technique used to make surfaces look old and worn

FAUX FINISHES
Painted finishes creating a false or simulated effect of some other material such as marble or wood

GESSO
A white chalky substance applied over a rough surface in order to give a smooth finish. Traditionally a base for gilding

GILDING
A technique for applying very thin leaves of gold to a surface. The term can also be used when using a metal-based leaf, sometimes called Dutch metal

GOLD SIZE
An adhesive used in the laying of gold leaf or metal leaf. It can be purchased in a range of drying times

GRISAILLE
A monochromatic palette, generally of blue and grey colours, often used for sculptural or architectural illustrations

ISOLATE
To separate one layer of material from another so that they cannot react with each other. This is normally done with shellac

JAPANNING
A term used by the English in the eighteenth century to describe the art of lacquering used to simulate lacquer work coming from the Orient

MASTIC
A term for the moulding material or 'stuffing' used in repoussé and moulage

MAT (matte)
A dull, non-glossy finish generally used when referring to varnish

MINERAL TURPENTINE
A solvent used with oil-based varnishes and paints, and as a brush cleaner

MITRE
To cut off a corner at a 45 degree angle

MOULAGE
The moulding and shaping of paper, which is then supported by a mastic so that the edges of prints are raised and free of the surface on which they are placed

MOULD
To press and shape as in sculpting

PALETTE
A range of colours used by an artist

PATINA
A soft mellowing of a surface normally caused by ageing

PRIMARY COLOURS
Red, yellow, blue

PVA
Polyvinyl acetate. A white, fast-drying, strong glue

REPOUSSÉ
The shaping and sculpting of paper which is supported by a mastic. The edges of the prints are adhered to the surface on which they are placed

SANDPAPER
An abrasive paper which comes in varying degrees of coarseness. The lower its number, the coarser the paper

SANGUINE
The name given to a palette in blood colours

SCALPEL
A surgeon's knife, with replaceable blades used in découpage for very intricate cutting

SECONDARY COLOURS
The result of mixing two primary colours

SHELLAC
A resinous varnish used in découpage as a sealer and isolator. It is used with methylated spirits

SINGERIE
Whimsical illustrations depicting monkeys in a decorative form

TEMPLATE
A copy or pattern usually made in cardboard or paper

TÔLE
Raised three-dimensional cut-outs

TORCHON
Paper pencil used for blending pastels or charcoal

TORTILLONS
Thick paper rolled into the shape of a pencil with a similar pointed end. They come in various sizes

WET-AND-DRY
A sandpaper which can be used wet or dry to achieve a smooth porcelain-like finish

WIRE/STEEL WOOL
An abrasive which comes in various degrees of coarseness and is used for final polishing. The finest grade 0000 is the one that should be used

X-ACTO KNIFE
A sharp craft knife with a fine point used for intricate cutting

Brand Names of Materials

CRAFT KNIVES
Swann Morton
X-Acto

COLOURED PENCILS
Berol Karismacolor

GESSO
Daler-Rowney
Liquitex

GLUE
Evo-Stick Fabric Adhesive
Evo-Stick Paper Glue
Gloy
Polycell Wallpaper Paste
PrittStick Paper Glue
PVA White Glue

MASTIC
DAS Modelling Clay
Plasticine

PAINTS
Daler-Rowney
Liquitex
Winsor & Newton

REMOVABLE ADHESIVES
Bostik Blu-Tack

SCISSORS
Diamond Edge
Wilkinsons

SEALERS
Liquitex Gloss Medium & Varnish
Liquitex Matte Varnish
Winsor & Newton Spray Fixative

TACK CLOTHS
Halfords

VARNISHES
Oil-based
Ronseal

Water-based
Cuprinol Enhance Clear Acrylic
Liquitex
Masters Acrylic Finish

WOOD FILLERS
Cuprinol
Ronseal

Further information about the craft of découpage in the United Kingdom can be obtained from the following address:

The Secretary
National Guild of Découpeurs
(English Chapter)
The Cottage
Barton End House
Bath Road
Nailsworth
Gloucestershire
GL6 0QQ

Bibliography

Davis, Dee and Frenkel, Dee, *Step-by-Step Découpage*, Golden Press, New York, 1976.

Découpage Guild Australia, Inc., P.O. Box 395, Malvern, Victoria, 3144.

Dover Publications Inc. (various titles), 180 Varick Street, New York, New York, USA.

Hayden, Ruth, *Mrs Delaney, her life and flowers*, British Museum Publications, London, 1980.

Ladies Amusement Book or The Whole Art of Japanning Made Easy. Facsimile of the original edition published for Robert Sayers at the Golden Buck, 53 Fleet Street, London in 1760. Ceramic Book Company, Newport, Wales, 1959.

Manning, Maybelle, 'Découpage: Hobby or Vice?', *American Home*, January 1949, p. 46.

Manning, Hiram, *Manning on Découpage*, Dover Publications, Hearthside Publications Inc., New York, 1969.

Mitchell, Marie, *The Art of Découpage*, Marie Mitchell's Découpage Center, Detroit, 1966.

Mitchell, Marie, *Advanced Découpage*, Marie Mitchell's Découpage Center, Detroit, 1969.

National Guild of Découpeurs, 807 Rivard Boulevard, Grosse Point, Michigan 48230, USA.

Newman, Thelma R., *Contemporary Découpage*, Crown Publications Inc., New York, 1972.

Nimmocks, Patricia, *Découpage*, Charles Scribners Sons, New York, 1968.

Wakefield, David, *French Eighteenth Century Painting*, Gordon Fraser, London, 1984.

Wing, Frances S., *The Complete Book of Découpage*, Coward, McCann and Geoghegan, New York, 1965.

Index

Numbers in italics refer to photographs. While the découpeurs who have created works reproduced in this book have been included in the index, please check the Acknowledgments for details of the relevant pieces of work.

acrylics, 18, 88
air bubbles
  under glass, 49
  under prints, 22
air, clean, 22
Allbright, Joy, *60, 67*
antiquing, 26
art deco, 33
art deco and art nouveau prints, colouring, 70
art nouveau, 33, 88
art povera, 10
art del povera, 10

Barbour, Philippa, *66*
Baroque, 31, 88
Biedermeier, 13, 88
bisque découpage, *80,* 80–81
Blackburn, Amelia, 12–13
Blinkhorn, Susan, *71*
Boucher, François, 10, 11
Boucher, Palette, 66
Bowden, Kristine, *45*
boxes, wooden
  interior treatment, 38–39
  lining, 45–46, 54–57
brand names of materials, 91
brayer, 88
bread dough, 17–18
British Museum, 12
brushes, care of, 27–28, 38
burnisher, 72, 73, *73,* 74
Byzantine, 88

Cant, Phyllis, *52*
carnauba, 88
cartouche, 88
chinagraph pencil, 88
chinoiserie, 11, 15, 31
Chinoiserie Palette, 66
chips, 22
classicism, 15

cloisonné, 15, 58–59, *60*
colour, 32–33
  cool and warm, 64–65
colour pencils, 16
colour wheel, 65
colouring *see* hand colouring
complementary colours, 64–65, 88
Cooper, June, *76*
crackle, 88
creative cutting, 14, 15
Cullen, Nerida, *62, 71, 78*
cut-outs
  overlapping, 43
  picking up, 26
  positioning, 33–34, 41, *41*
    under glass, 48–49, *49*
  selecting, 34
cutting back and polishing, 44
cutting out, 24–25, 39–40, *39*
  cloisonné, 59, *59*

découpage, 8–9, 10, 68
  on wood box, 37
  under glass, 47–53, *51, 52*
  under varnish, 36–46, *44, 45*
découpeur, 88
Delaney, Mrs, 12–13
dents, 22
design, 31–35, *41,* 48
distressing, 26, 88
drying, 22–23, 25
Duer, Caroline, 13–14
dust free environment, 22–23, 42
Dutch metal (gold metal leaf), 83, 85

Eighteenth Century Palette, 66
Empire Palette, 66
Empress Josephine, 11, 66
Erté, *37*

faux finishes, 88
Fink, Margaret, 44

Fragonard, 10
Frank, Jean-Michel, 13
Furze, Faye, *52*

gesso, 16–17, 37, 52, 53, 88
gilding, 89
glass
  backgrounds for, 50–53, *50, 51*
  cleaning, 48
  découpage, 47–53, *51, 52*
  drying, 25
gloss finishes, 25
gluing, 41–42
gold leaf transparency, 82–85, *84*
gold size, 89
Grisaille Palette, 67, 89

hand colouring, 64–71, *66, 67, 69–71*
  technique, 67–68
  traditional, 68–69
hinged boxes
  painting, 38
  support, 29
history and styles of découpage, 10–15
Hughes, Mark (cutting), *44*

illumination, 15, 60–63, *60–62*
intermediary colours, 64
isolating, 69

japanning, 10, 89

lacche povera, 10
lacche (lacca) contrafatta, 10, *11*
lacque pauvre, 10
Lade, Val, *80*
l'art scriban, 10
lining a box
  round, 45–46, 56–57
  square or rectangular, 54–56
Luget, Judith, *83*
lumps, 22

Manning, Hiram, 14, 66
Manning, Maybelle, 14
Marie Antoinette, 11
mastic, 17, 72, 74, *74*, 75, *75*, 89
mat (matte), 89
materials, 16–21, *17*
  basic, 36
  cloisonné, 50

glass découpage, 47–48
hand colouring, 68, 70
illumination, 60–61
lined box, 54
repoussé, 72
Matisse, Henri, 13
McNickle, Lola, *32, 45, 83, 84*
mineral turpentine, 89
mirror découpage 81, *81*
mitre, 89
moiré, 30
Morris, William, 33
mother of pearl inlay, *14*
moulage, 15, 72, *73*, 75–76, *75–77*, 89
moulding material, 17–18
mulberry paper, 50

National Guild of Découpeurs, The (USA) *12*, 14, *14*, 15, *15*, 33, 48, *66*, *73*, *79*, *81*
Neoclassicism, 33
Nimmocks, Patricia, 13, 66

oil and water, 16
oil-based paints, 18
oil-based sanding sealer, 43
oil-based varnishes, 18, 21, 43
oriental woodblocks, colouring, 70

painted backgrounds, 26
  under glass, 51–53
painted effects, 53
painting
  the edges of prints, 40, *40*
  a wood box, 38
paints, 18
palette, 89
paper
  collecting and storing, 23–24
  glass background, 50–51
  glass découpage, 46
  thinning, 29–30
  torn, 30
patina, 89
perspective, 35, 68
Picasso, Pablo, 13
Pillement, 10, 11, 12, *14, 66*
polishing, 27, 44
Pompadour, Madame de, 11
Pompadour Palette, 66
porcelain découpage, 79–80

Potichomania, 47
pre-varnished and pre-painted objects, 27
primary colours, 64, 89
prints *see* cut-outs
proportion, 33
Provincial Garden Palette, 66
PVA (polyvinyl acetate), 89

Raymond, Audrey, *37, 44, 45, 51, 52, 60, 78, 84*
Redouté, Pierre, 10, 11
repoussé, 15, 72–77, *73–74, 76*, 89
rice paper, 50
Roman bureau, *11*
Romanticism, 33
Royal College of Art, 31
rust, 28

sanding, 28–29, 43, 44
  a wood box, 37
sandpapers, 18, 89
Sanguine Palette, 67, 89
Sartor, Joanne, *14*
Sayer, Robert
  The Ladies Amusement or Whole Art of Japanning Made Easy, 11–12
scalpel, 42, 90
scissors, 24, 29
sealers, 18–19
  oil-based sanding, 43
sealing a wood box, 37–38
secondary colours, 64, 90
selecting prints, 34–35, 39
shades, 66
shell découpage, 82, *83*
shellac, 19, 90
  brush cleaning, 28
silk découpage, 78–79, *78–79*
singerie, 11, 90
Singleton, Nerida, *13*

smoked glass, 53
soap découpage, 81–82
stains, 19
surfaces, 19–20, *20*

tack cloths, 25–26, 36
techniques and tips, 22–30
template, 90
tertiary colours, 64
tints, 65
Toile de Jouey Palette, 66–67
tôle 15, *76, 77*, 90
torchon, 90
tortillons, 90
toxic fumes and dust, 30
triptych screen, *62*

varnish
  crazed or wrinkled, 24
  milky bloom on, 26
  sanding through, 28–29
  water marked, 30
varnishes, 20–21
varnishing, *42*, 42–44
  repoussé and moulage, 76–77
Victoria, Queen, 13, 31
vue d'optique, 15, *15*

water-based paints, 18
water-based varnishes, 18, 20
water marks, 30
Watteau, 10
wet-and-dry sandpapers, 18, 90
wet sanding, 43, 44
White, Dorothy, *45*, 76
wire/steel wool, 90

x-acto knife, 90